STEPHEN ARTERBURN

100 DAYS OF
CHARACTER
STRONG ROOTS FOR A STRONG LIFE

NewLife Ministries

*The quoted ideas expressed in this book (but not Scripture verses) are not, in all cases, exact quotations, as some have been edited
for clarity and brevity. In all cases, the author has attempted to maintain the speaker's original intent. In some cases, quoted
material for this book was obtained from secondary sources, primarily print media. While every effort was made to ensure the
accuracy of these sources, the accuracy cannot be guaranteed. For additions, deletions, corrections, or clarifications in future
editions of this text, please write New Life Ministries.*

Scripture quotations are taken from:

Scriptures marked NIV® are from the Holy Bible, New International Version®. Copyright © 1973, 1978, 1984 by
International Bible Society. Used by permission of Zondervan Publishing House. All rights reserved.

Scriptures marked NASB are taken from the New American Standard Bible®. © Copyright The Lockman Foundation
1960, 1962, 1963, 1968, 1971, 1972, 1973, 1975, 1977, 1995. Used by permission. (www.Lockman.org).

Scriptures marked NKJV are taken from the New King James Version®. Copyright © 1982 by Thomas Nelson, Inc.
Used by permission. All rights reserved.

Scriptures marked NLT are taken from the Holy Bible, New Living Translation, copyright © 1996. Used by permission
of Tyndale House Publishers, Inc., Wheaton, Illinois 60189. All rights reserved.

Scriptures marked NCV are quoted from The Holy Bible, New Century Version, copyright © 1987, 1988, 1991 by
Word Publishing, Nashville, TN 37214. Used by permission.

Scriptures marked KJV are taken from the King James Version.

Scripture quotations marked MSG are taken from The Message. Copyright © by Eugene H. Peterson 1993, 1994,
1995. Used by permission of NavPress Publishing Group.

Scripture quotations marked HCSB are taken from the Holman Christian Standard Bible ®, Copyright © 1999, 2000,
2002, 2003 by Holman Bible Publishers. Used by permission. Holman Christian Standard Bible®, Holman CSB®, and
HCSB® are federally registered trademarks of Holman Bible Publishers.

Cover Design by Kevin Doherty
Page Layout by Bart Dawson

ISBN 978-1-58334-493-4

Printed in the United States of America

Introduction

Sometimes it seems that life here in the 21st century has been designed with an overriding purpose in mind: to test—and if possible, to tear down—your character. At almost every turn, you are tempted to take shortcuts, to follow the wrong role models, and to betray your conscience. If you fall prey to these temptations, you will inevitably disappoint your family, your community, and yourself. A far better strategy, of course, is to guard your integrity like you guard your wallet, and this book is intended to help.

This text contains 100 devotional readings that are intended to remind you of the importance of character: keeping it, building it, and passing it on to the next generation. So, for the next 100 days, do yourself and your loved ones a big-league favor: read a chapter a day and internalize the ideas that you find here.

This text contains Biblically-based prescriptions for the inevitable challenges that accompany life-here-on-earth. As you consider your own circumstances, remember this: whatever the size of your challenge, whatever the scope of your temptation or your problem, God is bigger. Much bigger. He will instruct you, protect you, energize you, and heal you if you let Him. So let Him. Pray fervently, listen carefully, work diligently, and treat every single day as an exercise in character-building, because that's precisely what every day can be . . . and should be.

100 DAYS OF CHARACTER-BUILDING

Blessed is the man who walks not in the counsel of the ungodly, nor stands in the path of sinners, nor sits in the seat of the scornful; but his delight is in the law of the Lord, and in His law he meditates day and night. He shall be like a tree planted by the rivers of water, that brings forth its fruit in its season, whose leaf also shall not wither; and whatever he does shall prosper.

PSALM 1:1-3 NKJV

You're about to begin a 100-day journey, an exploration of your character: what it is at this moment, what it should be today, and what it can become tomorrow. During the next 100 days, you will be challenged to examine your habits, your thoughts, your priorities, and your behaviors. And you'll be challenged to consider proven formulas for character-building, strategies for making the most of the talents and the opportunities that have been given to you by your Creator.

Catherine Marshall correctly observed, "The single most important element in any human relationship is honesty—with oneself, with God, and with others." Yet all too often, we find it far more convenient to be dishonest with ourselves, with our loved ones, and with our Father in heaven. And the results can be heartbreaking.

As Christians we are called to walk with God and to obey His commandments. But, we live in a world that presents us with countless temptations to wander far from God's path. These temptations have the potential to destroy us, in part, because they cause us to be dishonest with ourselves and with others.

Dishonesty is a habit. Once we start bending the truth, we're likely to keep bending it. A far better strategy, of course, is to acquire the habit of being completely forthright with God, with other people, and with ourselves.

Honesty, like its counterpart, is also a habit, a habit that pays powerful dividends for those who place character above convenience. So, for the next 100 days, make this simple promise to yourself and keep it: when you're tempted to bend the truth, even slightly—or to break it—ask yourself this question: "What does God want me to do?" Then listen carefully to your conscience. When you do, your actions will be honorable, and your character will take care of itself.

No man can use his Bible with power unless he has the character of Jesus in his heart.

ALAN REDPATH

CHARACTER BUILDER

Take time to think about your own character, both your strong points and your weaknesses. Then list three aspects of your character—longstanding habits or troublesome behaviors— that you would like to modify during the next 100 days. Finally, ask God to be your partner as you take steps to improve yourself and your life.

DAY 2

BUILDING CHARACTER BY PUTTING GOD FIRST

The thing you should want most is God's kingdom and doing what God wants. Then all these other things you need will be given to you.

The best way to build character—and the surest way—is to do it with God as your partner. So here's a question worth thinking about: Have you made God a full partner in your life's journey? Or are you in the habit of giving God little more than a few hours on Sunday morning? The answer to this question will determine, to a surprising extent, the direction of your day and the condition of your character.

As you contemplate your own relationship with the Creator, remember this: Everybody, without exception, is engaged in the practice of worship. Some folks choose to worship God and, as a result, reap the rewards that He has promised. Other folks who seem determined to do it "their way," inadvertently distance themselves from God, and from the path He intends for them to follow . . . and when they do, they suffer.

In the book of Exodus, God warns that we should place no gods before Him (20:3). Yet all too often, we place Him in second, third, or fourth place as we allow ourselves to be sidetracked by the temptations, addictions, and distractions that are woven into the fabric of 21st-century life.

Are you working to keep God first in your life? Do you talk with Him seven days a week, not just on Sunday mornings? And do you make big decisions after you've consulted Him, not before? Make certain that the honest answer to all these questions is a resounding yes. If you sincerely wish to build your character and your life on an unshakable foundation, you must put your Creator in first place. No exceptions.

We become whatever we are committed to.

RICK WARREN

Our ultimate aim in life is not to be healthy, wealthy, prosperous, or problem free. Our ultimate aim in life is to bring glory to God.

ANNE GRAHAM LOTZ

God calls us to be committed to Him, to be committed to making a difference, and to be committed to reconciliation.

BILL HYBELS

CHARACTER BUILDER

Think about your priorities. Are you really putting God first in your life, or are you putting other things— things like possessions, pleasures, or personal status—ahead of your relationship with the Father? And if your priorities for life are misaligned, think of at least three things you can do today to put God where He belongs: in first place.

THE RIGHT KIND OF EXAMPLE?

You should be an example to the believers in speech, in conduct, in love, in faith, in purity.

1 TIMOTHY 4:12 HCSB

Today, let's think about being roles models. And whether we admit it or not, we're all role models. Our friends and family members watch how we behave, and they make careful mental notes about what those behaviors say about the content of our character. So, if we want to be positive role models, we must try, as best we can, to insure that the things we say are congruent with the things we do. After all, our proclamations will never ring true unless we ourselves are willing to live by them.

What kind of example are you? Are you the kind of person whose life serves as a model of integrity and decency? Are you a positive role model for kids of all ages? Are you the kind of person whose actions, day in and day out, are determined by what's right, not what's expedient? If so, you are destined to be a powerful force for good in a world that desperately needs positive influences such as yours.

Phillips Brooks advised, "Be such a man, and live such a life, that if every person were such as you, and every life a life like yours, this earth would be God's Paradise." That's sound advice because your family and friends are watching carefully . . . and so, for that matter, is God.

We urgently need people who encourage and inspire us to move toward God and away from the world's enticing pleasures.

JIM CYMBALA

In your desire to share the gospel, you may be the only Jesus someone else will ever meet. Be real and be involved with people.

BARBARA JOHNSON

In our faith we follow in someone's steps. In our faith we leave footprints to guide others. It's the principle of discipleship.

MAX LUCADO

A holy life will produce the deepest impression. Lighthouses blow no horns; they only shine.

D. L. MOODY

CHARACTER BUILDER

Your life is a sermon. What kind of sermon will you preach?
The words you choose to speak may have some impact on others,
but not nearly as much impact as the life you choose to live.
Today, pause to consider the tone, the theme, and the context
of your particular sermon, and ask yourself if
it's a message that you're proud to deliver.

Faith Builds Character

I assure you: If anyone says to this mountain, "Be lifted up and thrown into the sea," and does not doubt in his heart, but believes that what he says will happen, it will be done for him.

Mark 11:23 HCSB

Because we live in a demanding world, all of us have mountains to climb and mountains to move. Moving those mountains requires faith. And the experience of trying, with God's help, to move mountains builds character.

Faith, like a tender seedling, can be nurtured or neglected. When we nurture our faith through prayer, meditation, and worship, God blesses us, He lifts our spirits, and He leads us in the right direction. But when we neglect the spiritual side of life, we do ourselves and our loved ones a disservice.

Are you a mountain-moving person whose faith is evident for all to see? Or, are you a spiritual underachiever? As you think about the answer to that question, consider this: God needs more people who are willing to move mountains for His glory and for His kingdom.

Every life—including yours—is a series of wins and losses. Every step of the way, through every triumph and tragedy, God walks with you, ready and willing to strengthen you. So the next time you find your character being tested, remember to take your fears to God. If you call upon Him, you will be comforted. Whatever your challenge, whatever your trouble, God can handle it.

When you place your faith, your trust, indeed your life in the hands of your Heavenly Father, you'll receive a lesson in character-building from the ultimate Teacher. So strengthen your faith through praise, through worship, through Bible study, and through prayer. And trust God's plans. With Him, all things are possible, and He stands ready to open a world of possibilities to you . . . if you have faith.

Faith is confidence in the promises of God or confidence that God will do what He has promised.

CHARLES STANLEY

Only God can move mountains, but faith and prayer can move God.

E. M. BOUNDS

I do not want merely to possess a faith; I want a faith that possesses me.

CHARLES KINGSLEY

CHARACTER BUILDER

Today, think about the times you've been hesitant to share your faith. And as you contemplate the day ahead, think about three specific ways that you can vocalize your faith to family and friends.

A WORLD BRIMMING WITH TEMPTATION

Be careful! Watch out for attacks from the Devil, your great enemy. He prowls around like a roaring lion, looking for some victim to devour. Take a firm stand against him, and be strong in your faith.

1 PETER 5:8-9 NLT

It's inevitable: today you will be tempted by somebody or something—in fact, you will probably be tempted on countless occasions. Why? Because you live in a world that's filled to the brim with temptations and addictions that are intended to lead you far, far away from God.

Here in the 21st century, temptations are now completely and thoroughly woven into the fabric of everyday life. Seductive images are everywhere; subtle messages tell you that it's okay to sin "just a little"; and to make matters even worse, society doesn't just seem to endorse godlessness, it actually seems to reward it. Society spews forth a wide range of messages, all of which imply that it's okay to rebel against God. These messages, of course, are extremely dangerous and completely untrue.

How can you stand up against society's tidal wave of temptations? By learning to direct your thoughts and your eyes toward things that are pleasing to God . . . and by relying upon Him to help you stay focused on things that are "whatever is honorable, whatever is just, whatever is pure, whatever is lovely, whatever is commendable" (Philippians 4:8). And here's the good news: the Creator has promised (not implied, not suggested, not insinuated—He has promised!) that with His help, you can resist every single temptation that confronts you.

Once you firmly decide to stand up to temptation, you are never alone. God is always with you, and if you do your part, He will do His part. But what, precisely, is your part? A good starting point is simply learning how to recognize the subtle temptations that surround you. The images of immorality are ubiquitous, and they're intended to hijack your mind, your heart, your pocketbook, your life, and your soul. Don't let them do it.

Most Christians do not know or fully realize that the adversary of our lives is Satan and that his main tool is our flesh, our old nature.

BILL BRIGHT

The first step on the way to victory is to recognize the enemy.

CORRIE TEN BOOM

CHARACTER BUILDER

Ask yourself these important questions: What images, people, or places are you likely to encounter today that might encourage you to think impure thoughts? And how will you prepare yourself to respond to these temptations?

DISCIPLINE BUILDS CHARACTER

But I discipline my body and bring it into subjection, lest, when I have preached to others, I myself should become disqualified.

1 CORINTHIANS 9:27 NKJV

Character and discipline go hand-in-hand. It takes discipline to build strong character and discipline to keep it. Perhaps that's why the Bible reminds us again and again that we should do our best to lead disciplined lives.

The world doesn't reward laziness, misbehavior, apathy, or addictive behaviors. To the contrary, if we want to earn big rewards from life, we have to earn them—the hard way—with dignity and discipline. But ours is a world in which dignity and discipline are often in short supply.

We live in a world in which sloppiness is often glorified, intemperance is sometimes glamorized, and addictions are often ignored . . . with predictably unfortunate results. God, however, has other plans for us. Proverbs 23:12 instructs: "Apply your heart to discipline and your ears to words of knowledge" (NASB). And, 2 Peter 1:5-6 teaches, "Make every effort to supplement your faith with goodness, goodness with knowledge, knowledge with self-control, self-control with endurance, endurance with godliness" (HCSB). Thus, God's Word is clear: we should exercise self-discipline in all matters. Otherwise, our talents are wasted and our resources are squandered.

Life's greatest rewards seldom fall into our laps; to the contrary, our greatest accomplishments usually require work, perseverance, and discipline. There simply are no shortcuts to any place worth going. May we, as thoughtful adults, behave ourselves accordingly.

If one examines the secret behind a championship football team, a magnificent orchestra, or a successful business, the principal ingredient is invariably discipline.

James Dobson

Simply stated, self-discipline is obedience to God's Word and willingness to submit everything in life to His will, for His ultimate glory.

John MacArthur

Personal humility is a spiritual discipline and the hallmark of the service of Jesus.

Franklin Graham

CHARACTER BUILDER

A disciplined lifestyle gives you more control:
The more disciplined you become, the more you can take
control over your life (which, by the way, is far better than
letting your life take control over you).

CHOICES THAT BUILD CHARACTER

I am offering you life or death, blessings or curses. Now, choose life!...
To choose life is to love the Lord your God, obey him, and stay close
to him.

DEUTERONOMY 30:19-20 NCV

Life is a series of choices. From the instant we wake up in the morning until the moment we nod off to sleep at night, we make countless decisions: decisions about the things we do, decisions about the words we speak, and decisions about the thoughts we choose to think. Simply put, the quality of those decisions determines the quality of our lives.

As believers who have been saved by a loving and merciful God, we have every reason to make wise choices. Yet sometimes, amid the inevitable hustle and bustle of life here on earth, we allow ourselves to behave in ways that we know are displeasing to our Creator. When we do, we forfeit the joy and the peace that we might otherwise experience through Him.

As you consider the next step in your life's journey, take time to consider how many things in this life you can control: your thoughts, your words, your priorities, and your actions, for starters. And then, if you sincerely want to discover God's purpose for your life, make choices that are pleasing to Him. He deserves no less ... and neither do you.

Sometimes, because you're an imperfect human being, you may become so wrapped up in meeting society's expectations that you fail to focus on God's expectations. To do so is a mistake of major proportions—don't make it. Instead, seek God's guidance as you focus your energies on becoming the best "you" that you can possibly be. And, when it comes to matters of conscience, seek approval not from your peers, but from your Creator.

Whom will you try to please today: God or man? Your primary obligation is not to please imperfect men and women. Your obligation is to strive diligently to meet the expectations of an all-knowing and perfect God. Trust Him always. Love Him always. Praise Him always. And make choices that please Him. Always.

Every day, I find countless opportunities to decide whether I will obey God and demonstrate my love for Him or try to please myself or the world system. God is waiting for my choices.

BILL BRIGHT

CHARACTER BUILDER

First you'll make choices . . . and before you know it, your choices will make you. So take time to think carefully about the direction of your life and the choices that you've been making. Then, try to come up with at least one "new and improved" choice that you can make today.

STUDYING GOD'S WORD BUILDS CHARACTER

You will be a good servant of Christ Jesus, constantly nourished on the words of the faith and of the sound doctrine which you have been following.

God's promises are found in a book like no other: the Holy Bible. The Bible is a roadmap for life here on earth and for life eternal. We are called upon to trust its promises, to follow its commandments, and to share its Good News. We are instructed to study the Bible each day and meditate upon its meaning for our lives. Otherwise, we deprive ourselves of an invaluable, character-building gift from the Creator. God's Holy Word is, indeed, a transforming, life-changing, one-of-a-kind treasure. And, a passing acquaintance with the Good Book is insufficient for those who seek to obey God's Word and to understand His will.

God has made promises to mankind and to you. God's promises never fail and they never grow old. You must trust those promises and share them with your family, with your friends, and with the world.

Are you standing on the promises of God? Are you expecting God to do wonderful things, or are you living beneath a cloud of apprehension and doubt? The familiar words of Psalm 118:24 remind us of a profound yet simple truth: "This is the day which the LORD hath made; we will rejoice and be glad in it" (KJV). Do you trust that promise, and do you live accordingly? If so, you are living the passionate life that God intends.

For passionate believers, every day begins and ends with God's Son and God's promises. As we face the inevitable challenges of life, we must arm ourselves with the promises of God's Holy Word. When we do, we can expect the best, not only for the day ahead, but also for all eternity.

Reading news without reading the Bible will inevitably lead to an unbalanced life, an anxious spirit, a worried and depressed soul.

BILL BRIGHT

God gives us a compass and a Book of promises and principles— the Bible—and lets us make our decisions day by day as we sense the leading of His Spirit. This is how we grow.

WARREN WIERSBE

CHARACTER BUILDER

Trust God's Word: Charles Swindoll writes, "There are four words I wish we would never forget, and they are, 'God keeps his word.'" And remember: When it comes to studying God's Word, school is always in session.

OPTIMISM BUILDS CHARACTER

I can do everything through him that gives me strength.

PHILIPPIANS 4:13 NIV

As each day unfolds, you are quite literally surrounded by more opportunities than you can count—opportunities to improve your own life and the lives of those you love. God's Word promises that you, like all of His children, possess the ability to experience earthly peace and spiritual abundance. Yet sometimes—especially if you dwell upon the inevitable disappointments that may, at times, befall even the luckiest among us—you may allow pessimism to invade your thoughts and your heart.

The 19th-century American poet Ella Wheeler Wilcox wrote a poem entitled "Optimism" in which she advised, "Say that you are well and all is well with you, and God will hear your words and make them true." Wilcox understood that optimism is, most often, a matter of intention. If you make the decision to think optimistically, if you purposefully direct your thoughts in positive directions, then you'll enhance your chances of achieving success.

It's undeniable: the self-fulfilling prophecy is alive, well, and living at your house. If you constantly anticipate the worst, that's what you're likely to attract. But, if you make the effort to think positive thoughts, you'll increase the probability that those positive thoughts will come true.

So here's a simple, character-building tip for improving your life: put the self-fulfilling prophecy to work for you. Expect the best, and then get busy working to achieve it. When you do, you'll not only increase the odds of achieving your dreams, but you'll also have more fun along the way.

The popular idea of faith is of a certain obstinate optimism: the hope, tenaciously held in the face of trouble, that the universe is fundamentally friendly and things may get better.

J. I. PACKER

It is a remarkable thing that some of the most optimistic and enthusiastic people you will meet are those who have been through intense suffering.

WARREN WIERSBE

CHARACTER BUILDER

Be a realistic optimist. Your attitude toward the future will help create your future. So think realistically about yourself and your situation while making a conscious effort to focus on hopes, not fears. When you do, you'll put the self-fulfilling prophecy to work for you.

ADVERSITY BUILDS CHARACTER

God is our refuge and strength, always ready to help in times of trouble. So we will not fear, even if earthquakes come and mountains crumble to the sea.

PSALM 46:1-2 NLT

As life here on earth unfolds, all of us encounter occasional disappointments and setbacks: Those occasional visits from Old Man Trouble are simply a fact of life, and none of us are exempt. When tough times arrive, we may be forced to rearrange our plans and our priorities. But even on our darkest days, we must never forget that God intends for us to use our setbacks as stepping stones on the path to a better life.

The fact that we encounter adversity is not nearly so important as the way we choose to deal with it. When tough times arrive, we have a clear choice: we can begin the difficult work of tackling our troubles . . . or not. When we summon the courage to look Old Man Trouble squarely in the eye, he usually blinks. But, if we refuse to address our problems, even the smallest annoyances have a way of growing into king-sized catastrophes.

Psalm 145 promises, "The Lord is near to all who call on him, to all who call on him in truth. He fulfills the desires of those who fear him; he hears their cry and saves them" (v. 18-20 NIV). And the words of Jesus offer us comfort: "These things I have spoken to you, that in Me you may have peace. In the world you will have tribulation; but be of good cheer, I have overcome the world" (John 16:33 NKJV).

In times of hardship, God will comfort us; in times of sorrow, He will dry our tears. When we are troubled or weak or sorrowful, the Father is always with us. We must build our lives on the rock that cannot be shaken: we must trust in God. And then, we must get on with the character-building, life-altering work of tackling our problems . . . because if we don't, who will? Or should?

Your greatest ministry will likely come out of your greatest hurt.

RICK WARREN

God will not permit any troubles to come upon us unless He has a specific plan by which great blessing can come out of the difficulty.

PETER MARSHALL

CHARACTER BUILDER

If you're having tough times, don't hit the panic button
and don't keep everything bottled up inside. Talk things over with
people you can really trust. A second opinion (or, for that matter,
a third, fourth, or fifth opinion) is usually helpful. So if your troubles
seem overwhelming, be willing to seek outside help—
starting, of course, with your pastor.

PRAYER BUILDS CHARACTER

And everything—whatever you ask in prayer, believing—you will receive.

MATTHEW 21:22 HCSB

In the battle to build character, prayer is an indispensable weapon. Your life is not a destination; it is a journey that unfolds day by day. And, that's exactly how often you should seek direction from your Creator: one day at a time, each day followed by the next, without exception.

Daily prayer and meditation is a matter of will and habit. When we carve out quiet moments with God, we soon discover that no time is more precious than the silent moments we spend with God.

God promises that the prayers of righteous men and women can accomplish great things (James 5:16). God promises that He answers prayer (although His answers are not always in accordance with our desires). God invites us to be still and to feel His presence. So pray. And pray often.

Is prayer an integral part of your daily life right now, or is it more of a a hit-or-miss routine? Do you "pray without ceasing," or is your prayer life little more than an afterthought? As you think about these questions, remember that the quality of your spiritual life will be in direct proportion to the quality of your prayer life.

Prayer changes things, and it changes you. Today, instead of turning things over in your mind, turn them over to God. Instead of worrying about your next decision, ask God to lead the way. Instead of struggling along against the inevitable temptations of everyday life, ask God to help you. Don't limit your prayers to meals or to bedtime; pray constantly. God is listening; He wants to hear from you; and you most certainly need to hear from Him.

When there is a matter that requires definite prayer, pray until you believe God and until you can thank Him for His answer.

HANNAH WHITALL SMITH

As we join together in prayer, we draw on God's enabling might in a way that multiplies our own efforts many times over.

SHIRLEY DOBSON

CHARACTER BUILDER

Prayer strengthens your character and your relationship
with God ... so pray. Martin Luther observed, "If I should neglect
prayer but a single day, I should lose a great deal of the fire of faith."
Those words apply to you, too. And it's up to you to live—
and to pray—accordingly.

FORGIVENESS NOW

Then Peter came to him and asked, "Lord, how often should I forgive someone who sins against me? Seven times?" "No!" Jesus replied, "seventy times seven!"

MATTHEW 18:21-22 NLT

It has been said that life is an exercise in forgiveness. And it should be added that forgiveness is also an exercise in character-building.

Christ understood the importance of forgiveness when he commanded, "Love your enemies and pray for those who persecute you" (Matthew 5:43-44 NIV). But sometimes, forgiveness is difficult indeed.

When we have been injured or embarrassed, we feel the urge to strike back and to hurt the ones who have hurt us. But Christ instructs us to do otherwise. Christ teaches us that forgiveness is God's way and that mercy is an integral part of God's plan for our lives. In short, we are commanded to weave the thread of forgiveness into the very fabric of our lives.

Do you invest more time than you should reliving the past? Are you troubled by feelings of anger, bitterness, envy, or regret? Do you harbor ill will against someone whom you simply can't seem to forgive? If so, it's time to finally get serious about forgiveness.

When someone hurts you, the act of forgiveness is difficult, but necessary. Until you forgive, you are trapped in a prison of your own creation. But what if you have tried to forgive and simply can't seem to do so? The solution to your dilemma is this: you simply must make forgiveness a higher priority in your life.

Most of us don't spend much time thinking about forgiveness; we worry, instead, about the injustices we have suffered and the people who inflicted them. God has a better plan: He wants us to live in the present, not the past, and He knows that in order to do so, we must forgive those who have harmed us.

Have you made forgiveness a high priority? Have you sincerely asked God to forgive you for your inability to forgive others? Have you genuinely prayed that those feelings of anger and resentment might be swept from your heart? If so, congratulations. If not, perhaps it's time to rearrange your priorities . . . and perhaps it's time to fortify your character by freeing yourself from the chains of bitterness and regret.

God expects us to forgive others as He has forgiven us; we are to follow His example by having a forgiving heart.

VONETTE BRIGHT

CHARACTER BUILDER

Today, make a list of the people you still need to forgive.
Then make up your mind to forgive at least one person on that list.
Finally, ask God to cleanse your heart of bitterness, animosity,
and regret. If you ask Him sincerely and often, He will respond.

THE NEED TO LEAD

Good leadership is a channel of water controlled by God; he directs it to whatever ends he chooses.

PROVERBS 21:1 MSG

Harry Truman was the plain-spoken American president who said, "If you can't stand the heat, get out of the kitchen." And, he spoke from hard-earned experience. As commander-in-chief during the final days of World War II, the feisty Mr. Truman faced many tough decisions, and he never dodged them. Instead, he followed the advice of another president, Andrew Jackson, who once said, "Take time to deliberate; but when the time for action arrives, stop thinking and go ahead."

If Truman were here, he'd be quick to say that genuine leadership is an exercise in character-building, not a popularity contest. Genuine leadership often requires tough decisions, decisions that by their definition, are displeasing to some. But, effective leaders are willing to sacrifice popularity for results.

If you occupy a position of leadership (and you do), then you should prepare yourself for the day when you will be faced with a tough, unpopular decision. When that day arrives, you have a choice to make: you can either do the right thing or the easy thing. Do the right thing. After all, every kitchen heats up on occasion, so you might as well get used to it. And, the best way to get used to a warm kitchen is to hang in there and take the heat, knowing that every kitchen, in time, cools down. And so will yours.

The test of a leader is taking the vision from me to we.

JOHN MAXWELL

What do we Christians chiefly value in our leaders? The answer seems to be not their holiness, but their gifts and skills and resources. The thought that only holy people are likely to be spiritually useful does not loom large in our minds.

J. I. PACKER

The goal of leadership is to empower the whole people of God to discern and to discharge the Lord's will.

STANLEY GRENZ

People who inspire others are those who see invisible bridges at the end of dead-end streets.

CHARLES SWINDOLL

CHARACTER BUILDER

Today, think about your own leadership style. Remember that leadership comes in many forms and that you will probably be more effective using your own style, not by trying to copy someone else. When it comes to leadership, an original version of yourself is far better than a weak imitation of someone else.

WHAT IS YOUR FOCUS?

Look straight ahead, and fix your eyes on what lies before you. Mark out a straight path for your feet; then stick to the path and stay safe. Don't get sidetracked; keep your feet from following evil.

PROVERBS 4:25-27 NLT

The condition of your character is determined, to a surprising extent, by the direction of your thoughts. If you focus your thoughts and energies on positive matters—if you focus on things that bring honor to your family and yourself—you'll reap rich rewards. But if you focus too intently on the distractions and temptations of our 21st-century world, you're inviting large quantities of trouble.

Paul Valéry observed, "We hope vaguely but dread precisely." How true. All too often, we allow the worries of everyday life to overwhelm our thoughts and cloud our vision. What's needed is a clearer perspective, a renewed faith, and a different focus.

When we focus on the frustrations of today or the uncertainties of tomorrow, we rob ourselves of peace in the present moment. But, when we focus on possibilities instead of roadblocks, our worries no longer tyrannize us.

What is your focus today? Are you willing to focus your thoughts and energies on God's blessings and upon His will for your life? Or will you turn your thoughts to other things? Before you answer that question, consider this: God created you in His own image, and He wants you to experience joy and abundance.

But, God will not force His joy upon you; you must claim it for yourself.

Today, remember that God is infinitely greater than the challenges that you face. Remember, too, that your thoughts are profoundly powerful, so guard them accordingly.

As long as Jesus is one of many options, he is no option.

MAX LUCADO

Just like commercial organizations need to get their focus off themselves, we as individual Christians and collective churches need to recalibrate our sights on the target God has given us: spiritually lost people.

BILL HYBELS

Only the man who follows the command of Jesus single-mindedly and unresistingly lets his yoke rest upon him, finds his burden easy, and under its gentle pressure receives the power to persevere in the right way.

DIETRICH BONHOEFFER

CHARACTER BUILDER

Ask yourself if you're truly focusing your thoughts and energies on matters that are pleasing to God and beneficial to your family. Then ask your Creator to help you focus on His love, His Son, and His plan for your life.

DAY 15

LIVING ON PURPOSE

For everything, absolutely everything, above and below, visible and invisible, rank after rank after rank of angels—everything got started in him and finds its purpose in him.

COLOSSIANS 1:16 MSG

Rosa Parks was a seamstress from Montgomery, Alabama, exhausted from a hard day's work, quietly riding home on a bus. But God had plans for her that were simply too big for Parks, or anyone else for that matter, to understand.

In 1955, African-Americans were expected to give up their seats and go to the back of the bus whenever a white rider or a bus driver ordered them to move. But on one fateful day, Rosa was told to move, and she refused. She was promptly arrested. This personal protest against injustice ignited the civil rights movement in Alabama and in America. And when she died in 2005, Rosa Parks became the first woman to lie in state in the U.S. Capitol rotunda. It was an honor that was, of course, richly deserved.

Whether you realize it or not, you're not that different from Rosa Parks: You can make big changes in your world if you summon the character-building courage to stand up for your beliefs. So if you're under the illusion that you're just one small person, and that you can't do big things for God, remember a former seamstress whose quiet dignity and fierce determination sparked a revolution. Then get busy looking for something you can change. When you do, you'll never take a back seat to anybody.

We must focus on prayer as the main thrust to accomplish God's will and purpose on earth. The forces against us have never been greater, and this is the only way we can release God's power to become victorious.

JOHN MAXWELL

Let us live with urgency. Let us exploit the opportunity of life. Let us not drift. Let us live intentionally. We must not trifle our lives away.

RAYMOND ORTLUND

When God speaks to you through the Bible, prayer, circumstances, the church, or in some other way, he has a purpose in mind for your life.

HENRY BLACKABY AND CLAUDE KING

CHARACTER BUILDER

Perhaps you're in a hurry to understand God's unfolding plan
for your life. If so, remember that God operates according
to a perfect timetable. That timetable is His, not yours.
So be patient. God has big things in store for you, but He may have
quite a few lessons to teach you before you are fully prepared
to do His will and fulfill His purpose.

BEYOND FEAR

I sought the Lord, and He answered me and delivered me from all my fears.

PSALM 34:4 HCSB

Eleanor Roosevelt observed, "You gain strength, courage and confidence every time you look fear in the face." And she was right—the decision to face a fear instead of running from it is always an exercise in character building.

We live in a world that can be, at times, a very frightening place. We live in a world that is, at times, a very discouraging place. We live in a world where life-changing losses can be so painful and so profound that it seems we will never recover. But, with God's help, and with the help of encouraging family members and friends, we can recover.

During the darker days of life, we are wise to remember the words of Jesus, who reassured His disciples, saying, "Take courage! It is I. Don't be afraid" (Matthew 14:27 NIV).

Are you willing to face your fears right now? Are you willing to cast off the chains of timidity and procrastination by deciding to do what needs to be done now, not "later"? If the answer to these questions is yes, then you're destined to build a better life for yourself and your loved ones.

Today, ask God for the courage to step beyond the boundaries of your self-doubts. Ask Him to guide you to a place where you can realize your full potential—a place where you are freed from the fear of failure. Ask Him to do His part, and promise Him that you will do your part. Don't ask Him to lead you to a "safe" place; ask Him to lead you to the "right" place . . . and remember: those two places are seldom the same.

When we meditate on God and remember the promises He has given us in His Word, our faith grows, and our fears dissolve.

CHARLES STANLEY

Worry is a cycle of inefficient thoughts whirling around a center of fear.

CORRIE TEN BOOM

The Lord Jesus by His Holy Spirit is with me, and the knowledge of His presence dispels the darkness and allays any fears.

BILL BRIGHT

CHARACTER BUILDER

Are you feeling anxious or fearful? If so, trust God to handle those problems that are simply too big for you to solve. Entrust the future—your future—to God. Then, spend a few minutes thinking about specific steps you can take to confront— and conquer—your fears.

DAY 17

HEALTHY RELATIONSHIPS BUILD CHARACTER

Do not be unequally yoked together with unbelievers. For what fellowship has righteousness with lawlessness? And what communion has light with darkness?

2 CORINTHIANS 6:14 NKJV

When you become involved in relationships that require you to compromise your values, you'll make yourself miserable. Why? Because emotional distress is contagious.

In a perfect world filled with perfect people, our relationships, too, would be perfect. But none of us are perfect and neither are our relationships . . . and that's okay. As we work to make our imperfect relationships a little happier and healthier, we grow as individuals and as families. But, if we find ourselves in relationships that are debilitating or dangerous, then changes must be made, and soon.

If you find yourself caught up in a personal relationship that is bringing havoc into your life, and if you can't seem to find the courage to do something about it, don't hesitate to consult your pastor. Or, you may seek the advice of a trusted friend or a professionally trained counselor. But whatever you do, don't be satisfied with the status quo.

God has grand plans for your life; He has promised you the joy and abundance that can be yours through Him. But to fully experience God's gifts, you need happy, emotionally healthy people to share them with. It's up to you to make sure that you do your part to build the kinds of relationships that will bring abundance to you, to your family, and to God's world.

Not everybody is healthy enough to have a front-row seat in your life.

SUSAN L. TAYLOR

Don't just grab at the first thing that comes along. Know when to refuse something that won't go anywhere.

WILL ROGERS

You are justified in avoiding people who send you from their presence with less hope and strength to cope with life's problems than when you met them.

ELLA WHEELER WILCOX

Show me a guy who can't say 'No,' and I'll show you a guy with lots of problems.

RED AUERBACH

CHARACTER BUILDER

Remember: It's tempting to follow the crowd,
but usually it's better to follow your conscience.

DAY 18

CHARACTER AND MATURITY

Don't become so well-adjusted to your culture that you fit into it without even thinking. Instead, fix your attention on God. You'll be changed from the inside out. Readily recognize what he wants from you, and quickly respond to it. Unlike the culture around you, always dragging you down to its level of immaturity, God brings the best out of you, develops well-formed maturity in you.

ROMANS 12:2 MSG

Character-building never happens overnight. To the contrary, the journey toward spiritual maturity lasts a lifetime. We should continue to grow and learn every day of our lives.

Norman Vincent Peale had the following advice for men and women of all ages: "Ask the God who made you to keep remaking you." That advice, of course, is perfectly sound, but often ignored.

When we cease to grow, either emotionally or spiritually, we do ourselves a profound disservice. But, if we study God's Word, if we obey His commandments, and if we live in the center of His will, we will not be "stagnant" believers; we will, instead, continue to mature . . . and that's exactly what we should strive to do.

Our lives and our characters are constructed by the countless thoughts and choices we make every day. Each day, we make decisions that can strengthen our character . . . or not. When we choose to honor the Creator with our thoughts, our prayers, and our actions, we keep growing day by day . . . and we are blessed day by day.

As I have continued to grow in my Christian maturity, I have discovered that the Holy Spirit does not let me get by with anything.

ANNE GRAHAM LOTZ

Being a Christian means accepting the terms of creation, accepting God as our maker and redeemer, and growing day by day into an increasingly glorious creature in Christ, developing joy, experiencing love, maturing in peace.

EUGENE PETERSON

Integrity and maturity are two character traits vital to the heart of a leader.

CHARLES STANLEY

CHARACTER BUILDER

Today, think about the quality of the choices that you've made recently. Are these choices helping you become a more mature Christian? If so, don't change. If not, think about the quality of your decisions, the consequences of those decisions, and the steps that you can take to make better decisions.

DAY 19

PATIENCE BUILDS CHARACTER

Be gentle to everyone, able to teach, and patient.

2 TIMOTHY 2:23 HCSB

The dictionary defines the word *patience* as "the ability to be calm, tolerant, and understanding." If that describes you, you can skip the rest of this page. But, if you're like most of us, you'd better keep reading.

For most of us, patience is a hard thing to master. Why? Because we have lots of things we want, and we know precisely when we want them: NOW (if not sooner). But our Father in heaven has other ideas; the Bible teaches that we must learn to wait patiently for the things that God has in store for us, even when waiting is difficult.

We live in an imperfect world inhabited by imperfect people. Sometimes, we inherit troubles from others, and sometimes we create troubles for ourselves. On other occasions, we see other people "moving ahead" in the world, and we want to move ahead with them. So we become impatient with ourselves, with our circumstances, and even with our Creator.

Psalm 37:7 instructs to "rest in the Lord, and wait patiently for Him" (NKJV). But, for most of us, waiting patiently for Him is hard. We are fallible beings who seek solutions to our problems today, not tomorrow. Still, God instructs us to wait patiently for His plans to unfold, and that's exactly what we should do.

Sometimes, patience is the price we pay for being responsible adults, and that's as it should be. After all, think how patient our Heavenly Father has been with us. So the next time you find yourself drumming your fingers as you wait for a quick resolution to the challenges of everyday living, take a deep breath and ask God for patience. Remember that patience builds character . . . and the best moment to start building is this one.

You can't step in front of God and not get in trouble. When He says, "Go three steps," don't go four.

CHARLES STANLEY

In all negotiations of difficulties, a man may not look to sow and reap at once. He must prepare his business and so ripen it by degrees.

FRANCIS BACON

CHARACTER BUILDER

The best things in life seldom happen overnight; they usually take time. Henry Blackaby writes, "The grass that is here today and gone tomorrow does not require much time to mature. A big oak tree that lasts for generations requires much more time to grow and mature. God is concerned about your life through eternity. Allow Him to take all the time He needs to shape you for His purposes. Larger assignments will require longer periods of preparation." How true.

YOU AND YOUR CONSCIENCE

If the way you live isn't consistent with what you believe, then it's wrong.

ROMANS 14:23 MSG

Billy Graham correctly observed, "Most of us follow our conscience as we follow a wheelbarrow. We push it in front of us in the direction we want to go." To do so, of course, is a profound mistake. Yet all of us, on occasion, have failed to listen to the voice that God planted in our hearts, and all of us have suffered the consequences of our choices.

God gave each of us a conscience for a very good reason: to listen to it. And if we're wise, we make it a practice to listen carefully to that quiet internal voice.

Few things in life torment us more than a guilty conscience. And, few things in life provide more contentment than the knowledge that we are obeying God's commandments. A clear conscience is one of the rewards we earn when we obey God's Word and follow His will. When we follow God's will and accept His gift of salvation, our earthly rewards are never-ceasing, and our heavenly rewards are everlasting.

So when your conscience speaks, listen and learn. In all likelihood, God is trying to get His message through. And in all likelihood, it is a message that you desperately need to hear.

To go against one's conscience is neither safe nor right. Here I stand. I cannot do otherwise.

MARTIN LUTHER

The convicting work of the Holy Spirit awakens, disturbs, and judges.

FRANKLIN GRAHAM

The beginning of backsliding means your conscience does not answer to the truth.

OSWALD SANDERS

He that loses his conscience has nothing left that is worth keeping.

IZAAK WALTON

Now the goal of our instruction is love from a pure heart, a good conscience, and a sincere faith.

1 TIMOTHY 1:5 HCSB

CHARACTER BUILDER

Today, remember this: the more important the decision …
the more carefully you should listen to your conscience.

WORSHIP BUILDS CHARACTER

Worship the Lord with gladness. Come before him, singing with joy. Acknowledge that the Lord is God! He made us, and we are his. We are his people, the sheep of his pasture.

PSALM 100:2-3 NLT

I f you want to build character, the church is a wonderful place to do it. Are you an active, contributing member of your local fellowship? The answer to this simple question will have a profound impact on the direction of your spiritual journey and the content of your character.

If you are not currently engaged in a local church, you're missing out on an array of blessings that include, but are certainly not limited to, the life-lifting relationships that you can—and should—be experiencing with fellow believers.

So do yourself a favor: Find a congregation you're comfortable with, and join it. And once you've joined, don't just attend church out of habit. Go to church out of a sincere desire to know and worship God. When you do, you'll be blessed by the men and women who attend your fellowship, and you'll be blessed by your Creator. You deserve to attend church, and God deserves for you to attend church, so don't delay.

Worship is our response to the overtures of love from the heart of the Father.

RICHARD FOSTER

God asks that we worship Him with our concentrated minds as well as with our wills and emotions. A divided and scattered mind is not effective.

CATHERINE MARSHALL

When God is at the center of your life, you worship. When he's not, you worry.

RICK WARREN

Worship is about rekindling an ashen heart into a blazing fire.

LIZ CURTIS HIGGS

Because his spiritual existence transcends form, matter, and location, we have the freedom to worship him and experience his indwelling presence wherever we are.

R. C. SPROUL

CHARACTER BUILDER

Worship reminds you of the awesome power of God. So worship Him daily, and allow Him to work through you every day of the week (not just on Sunday). The best way to worship God is to worship Him sincerely and often.

KINDNESS BUILDS CHARACTER

A kind man benefits himself, but a cruel man brings disaster on himself.

PROVERBS 11:17 HCSB

Kindness builds character just as surely as hatred destroys it. But kindness doesn't always come easy. When we are discouraged, tired, or afraid, we can scarcely summon the energy to utter a single kind word. But, God's commandment is clear: He intends that we make the conscious choice to treat others with kindness and respect, no matter our circumstances, no matter our emotions.

In the busyness and confusion of daily life, it is easy to lose focus, and it is easy to become frustrated. We are imperfect human beings struggling to manage our lives as best we can, but we often fall short. When we are distracted or disappointed, we may neglect to share a kind word or a kind deed. This oversight hurts others, but it hurts us most of all.

Today, slow yourself down and be alert for people who need your smile, your kind words, or your helping hand. Make kindness a centerpiece of your dealings with others. They will be blessed, and you will be, too.

When you weave the thread of kindness into the very fabric of your life, you'll be strengthening your character, but that's not all. You'll also be giving glory to the One who gave His life for you.

Be so preoccupied with good will that you haven't room for ill will.

E. Stanley Jones

When you extend hospitality to others, you're not trying to impress people, you're trying to reflect God to them.

Max Lucado

If we're to love people like we should, our hearts have to be as pleasant toward them as our appearances are. Otherwise, we're living a lie.

Mary Hunt

The mark of a Christian is that he will walk the second mile and turn the other cheek. A wise man or woman gives the extra effort, all for the glory of the Lord Jesus Christ.

John Maxwell

When you launch an act of kindness out into the crosswinds of life, it will blow kindness back to you.

Dennis Swanberg

CHARACTER BUILDER

As you plan for the day ahead, remember this:
kind words cost nothing, but when they're spoken at the right time,
they can be priceless.

MAKING THE MOST OF MISTAKES

Instead, God has chosen the world's foolish things to shame the wise, and God has chosen the world's weak things to shame the strong.

1 CORINTHIANS 1:27 HCSB

Everybody makes mistakes, and so will you. In fact, Winston Churchill once observed, "Success is going from failure to failure without loss of enthusiasm." What was good for Churchill is also good for you, too. You should expect to make mistakes—plenty of them—but you should not allow those missteps to rob you of the enthusiasm you need to fulfill God's plan for your life.

We are imperfect people living in an imperfect world; mistakes are simply part of the price we pay for being here. But, even though mistakes are an inevitable part of life's journey, repeated mistakes should not be. When we commit the inevitable blunders of life, we must correct them, learn from them, and pray for the wisdom not to repeat them. When we do, our mistakes become lessons, and our experiences become adventures in character-building.

When our shortcomings are made public, we may feel embarrassed or worse. We may presume (quite incorrectly) "everybody" is concerned with the gravity of our problem. And, as a consequence, we may feel the need to hide from our problems rather than confront them. To do so is wrong. Even when our pride is bruised, we must face up to our mistakes and seek to rise above them.

Have you made a king-sized blunder or two? Of course you have. But here's the big question: have you used your mistakes as stumbling blocks or stepping stones? The answer to this question will determine how well you perform in the workplace and in every other aspect of your life. So don't let the fear of past failures hold you back. Instead, do the character-building thing: own up to your mistakes and do your best to fix them. Remember: even if you've made a colossal blunder, God isn't finished with you yet—in fact, He's probably just getting started.

Truth will sooner come out of error than from confusion.

FRANCIS BACON

Lord, when we are wrong, make us willing to change; and when we are right, make us easy to live with.

PETER MARSHALL

I hope you don't mind me telling you all this. One can learn only by seeing one's mistakes.

C. S. LEWIS

CHARACTER BUILDER

Fix it sooner rather than later: When you make a mistake,
the time to make things better is now, not later!
The sooner you address your problem, the better. If not now, when?

A Life of Integrity

Better to be poor and honest than a rich person no one can trust.

PROVERBS 19:1 MSG

It has been said that character is what we are when nobody is watching. How true. But there's never really a time when nobody is watching because God is always around, and He's always paying attention. As Bill Hybels observed, "Every secret act of character, conviction, and courage has been observed in living color by our omniscient God." Yep, God sees all; He knows all—and all of us should behave accordingly.

Are you willing to guard your words and watch your steps? If so, you'll discover that living a life of integrity isn't always the easiest way, but it is always the right way.

So if you find yourself tempted to break the truth—or even to bend it—remember that honesty is God's policy . . . and it must also be yours. Simply put, if you really want to walk with God—and if you really want to guard your heart against the dangers of disobedience—you must protect your integrity even more carefully than you guard your wallet. When you do, your character will take care of itself . . . and you won't need to look over your shoulder to see who, besides God, is watching.

Integrity is not a given factor in everyone's life. It is a result of self-discipline, inner trust, and a decision to be relentlessly honest in all situations in our lives.

JOHN MAXWELL

A little lie is like a little pregnancy. It doesn't take long before everyone knows.

C. S. LEWIS

God doesn't expect you to be perfect, but he does insist on complete honesty.

RICK WARREN

Till I die, I will not deny my integrity. I will maintain my righteousness and never let go of it; my conscience will not reproach me as long as I live.

JOB 27:5-6 NIV

CHARACTER BUILDER

One of your greatest possessions is integrity ... don't lose it.
Billy Graham was right when he said: "Integrity is the glue that holds
our way of life together. We must constantly strive to keep
our integrity intact. When wealth is lost, nothing is lost; when health
is lost, something is lost; when character is lost, all is lost."

GOD GIVES US STRENGTH

Cast your burden on the Lord, and He will support you; He will never allow the righteous to be shaken.

PSALM 55:22 HCSB

It's a promise that is made over and over again in the Bible: Whatever "it" is, God can handle it.

Life isn't always easy. Far from it! Sometimes, life can seem like a long, tiring, character-building, fear-provoking journey. But even when the storm clouds form overhead, even during our darkest moments, we're protected by a loving Heavenly Father.

When we're worried, God can reassure us; when we're sad, God can comfort us. When our hearts are broken, God is not just near; He is here. So we must lift our thoughts and prayers to Him. When we do, He will answer our prayers. Why? Because He is our shepherd, and He has promised to protect us now and forever.

God's hand uplifts those who turn their hearts and prayers to Him. Will you count yourself among that number? Will you accept God's peace and wear God's armor against the temptations and distractions of our dangerous world? If you do, you can live courageously and optimistically, knowing that even on the darkest days, you and your Heavenly Father can handle every challenge you face, today and forever.

The next time you're disappointed, don't panic. Don't give up. Just be patient and let God remind you he's still in control.

MAX LUCADO

We do not understand the intricate pattern of the stars in their course, but we know that He Who created them does, and that just as surely as he guides them, He is charting a safe course for us.

BILLY GRAHAM

So rejoice! You are giving Him what He asks you to give Him—the chance to show you what He can do.

AMY CARMICHAEL

By ourselves we are not capable of suffering bravely, but the Lord possesses all the strength we lack and will demonstrate His power when we undergo persecution.

CORRIE TEN BOOM

You may not know what you are going to do; you only know that God knows what He is going to do.

OSWALD CHAMBERS

CHARACTER BUILDER

Today, think about ways that you can tap into God's strength:
try prayer, worship, and praise, for starters.

HABITS BECOME CHARACTER

Do not be deceived: "Evil company corrupts good habits."

1 CORINTHIANS 15:33 NKJV

It's an old saying and a true one: First, you make your habits, and then your habits make you. Some habits are character-builders, inevitably bringing you closer to God, while other habits will lead you away from the path He has chosen for you. If you sincerely desire to improve your spiritual health, you must honestly examine the habits that make up the fabric of your day. And you must abandon those habits that are displeasing to God.

Perhaps you've tried to become a more disciplined person, but you're still falling back into your old habits. If so, don't get discouraged. Instead, you should become even more determined to evolve into the person God wants you to be.

If you trust God, and if you keep asking for His help, He can transform your life. If you sincerely ask Him to help you, the same God who created the universe will help you defeat the harmful habits that have heretofore defeated you. So, if at first you don't succeed, keep praying. God is listening, and He's ready to help you become a better person if you ask Him . . . so ask today.

You will never change your life until you change something you do daily.

JOHN MAXWELL

The simple fact is that if we sow a lifestyle that is in direct disobedience to God's reveled Word, we ultimately reap disaster.

CHARLES SWINDOLL

Since behaviors become habits, make them work with you and not against you.

E. STANLEY JONES

He who does not overcome small faults, shall fall little by little into greater ones.

THOMAS À KEMPIS

Prayer is a habit. Worship is a habit. Kindness is a habit. And if you want to please God, you'd better make sure that these habits are your habits.

MARIE T. FREEMAN

CHARACTER BUILDER

Target your most unhealthy habit first, and attack it with vigor. When it comes to defeating harmful habitual behaviors, you'll need focus, determination, more focus, and more determination.

Listening to Guilt

There is therefore now no condemnation to those who are in Christ Jesus, who do not walk according to the flesh, but according to the Spirit.

Romans 8:1 NKJV

All of us have made mistakes. Sometimes, we are swept up by events that encourage us to behave in ways that we later come to regret. And sometimes, even when our intentions are honorable, we make errors in judgment that have long-lasting consequences. When we look back at our actions with remorse, we may experience intense feelings of guilt. But God has an answer for the guilt that we feel. That answer is His forgiveness.

Sometimes, long after God has forgiven us, we may continue to withhold forgiveness from ourselves. Instead of accepting God's mercy and accepting our past, we may think far too long and hard about the things that "might have been," the things that "could have been," or the things that "should have been."

Are you troubled by feelings of guilt, even after you've received God's forgiveness? Are you still struggling with painful memories of mistakes you made long ago? Are you focused so intently on yesterday that your vision of today is clouded? If so, you still have work to do—spiritual work. You should ask your Heavenly Father not for forgiveness (He granted that gift the very first time you asked Him!) but instead for acceptance and trust: acceptance of the past and trust in God's plan for your life.

If you find yourself plagued by feelings of guilt or shame, consult God's survival guide: His Holy Word. And as you do so, consider the following Biblically-based tips for overcoming those feelings of guilt once and for all:

1. Stop doing the things that make you feel guilty: How can you expect not to feel guilty if you should feel guilty? (Acts 26:20) 2. Ask God for forgiveness. When you ask for it, He will give it. (1 John 1:9) 3. Ask forgiveness from the people you have harmed: This step is hard, but helpful. And even if the other folks cannot find it in their hearts to forgive you, you have the satisfaction of knowing that you asked. (Proverbs 28:13) 4. Forgive yourself: if you're no longer misbehaving, it's the right thing to do. And today is the right day to do it. (Romans 14:22) 5. Become more diligent in your daily time of prayer and Bible study. A regular time of quiet reflection and prayer will allow you to praise your Creator, to focus your thoughts, to remind yourself of His love, and to seek His guidance in matters great and small. (Isaiah 50:4-5) 6. Get busy making the world a better place. Now that God has forgiven you, it's time for you to show your gratitude by serving Him. (Matthew 23:11-12)

Guilt is a gift that leads us to grace.

FRANKLIN GRAHAM

CHARACTER BUILDER

If you've asked for God's forgiveness, He has given it. But have you forgiven yourself? If not, the best moment to do so is this one.

PERSEVERANCE BUILDS CHARACTER

For you need endurance, so that after you have done God's will, you may receive what was promised.

HEBREWS 10:36 HCSB

As you continue to seek God's purpose for your life, you will undoubtedly experience your fair share of disappointments, detours, false starts, and failures. When you do, you're facing one of those inevitable tests of character. Don't become discouraged: God's not finished with you yet.

The old saying is as true today as it was when it was first spoken: "Life is a marathon, not a sprint." That's why wise travelers (like you) select a traveling companion who never tires and never falters. That partner, of course, is your Heavenly Father.

The next time you find your courage tested to the limit, remember that God is as near as your next breath, and remember that He offers strength and comfort to His children. He is your shield and your strength; He is your protector and your deliverer. Call upon Him in your hour of need and then be comforted. Whatever your challenge, whatever your trouble, God can help you persevere. And that's precisely what He'll do if you ask Him.

Perhaps you are in a hurry for God to help you resolve your difficulties. Perhaps you're anxious to earn the rewards that you feel you've already earned from life. Perhaps you're drumming your fingers, impatiently waiting for God to act. If so, be forewarned:

God operates on His own timetable, not yours. Sometimes, God may answer your prayers with silence, and when He does, you must patiently persevere. In times of trouble, you must remain steadfast and trust in the merciful goodness of your Heavenly Father. Whatever your problem, He can manage it. Your job is to keep persevering until He does.

Jesus taught that perseverance is the essential element in prayer.

E. M. BOUNDS

Just remember, every flower that ever bloomed had to go through a whole lot of dirt to get there!

BARBARA JOHNSON

Perseverance is more than endurance. It is endurance combined with absolute assurance and certainty that what we are looking for is going to happen.

OSWALD CHAMBERS

CHARACTER BUILDER

Are you being tested? Call upon God. God can give you
the strength to persevere, and that's exactly
what you should ask Him to do.

FRIENDS WHO HELP YOU STRENGTHEN YOUR CHARACTER

As iron sharpens iron, a friend sharpens a friend.

The dictionary defines the word "friend" as "a person who is attached to another by feelings of affection or personal regard." This definition is accurate, as far as it goes, but when we examine the deeper meaning of friendship, many more descriptors come to mind: trustworthiness, loyalty, helpfulness, kindness, understanding, forgiveness, encouragement, humor, and cheerfulness, to mention but a few. Needless to say, our trusted friends and family members can help us discover God's unfolding purposes for our lives. Our task is to enlist our friends' wisdom, their cooperation, their honesty, and their encouragement.

If you genuinely want to strengthen your character, you need to build closer relationships with people who want to do the same. That's why fellowship with likeminded believers should be an integral part of your life. Your friendships should be uplifting, enlightening, encouraging, and (above all) character-building.

Are your friends the kind of people who encourage you to seek God's will and to obey God's Word? If so, you're choosing your friends wisely.

When you build lasting friendships that are pleasing to God, friendships with godly men and women whose values are admirable and whose intentions are honorable, you will be richly blessed. But if you find yourself spending time with folks whose priorities are as questionable as their ethics, you're treading on dangerous ground. So here's an invaluable tip for character building: be careful, very careful, how you choose your friends.

As you're making friendships, be less concerned with appearances and more concerned with integrity. Resolve to be a trustworthy, encouraging, loyal friend to others. And make sure that you appreciate the genuine friends who, by their presence and their love, make you a better person. Friendship is, after all, a glorious gift, praised by God. Give thanks for that gift and nurture it.

Inasmuch as anyone pushes you nearer to God, he or she is your friend.

BARBARA JOHNSON

God often keeps us on the path by guiding us through the counsel of friends and trusted spiritual advisors.

BILL HYBELS

CHARACTER BUILDER

Today, as you think about the nature and the quality of your friendships, remember the first rule of making (and keeping) friends: it's the Golden Rule, and it starts like this: "Do unto others . . . ."

ENTHUSIASM, PROPERLY DIRECTED, BUILDS CHARACTER

Whatever you do, do it enthusiastically, as something done for the Lord and not for men.

COLOSSIANS 3:23 HCSB

Are you enthusiastic about character-building and about life-building? Are you passionate about building your life on a foundation of faith and integrity? And are you excited about your faith, your family, and your future? If so, congratulations, and keep up the good work! But, if your spiritual batteries are running low, perhaps you're spending too much energy focusing on your losses and too little time planning for future victories.

Norman Vincent Peale advised, "Get absolutely enthralled with something. Throw yourself into it with abandon. Get out of yourself. Be somebody. Do something." His words apply to you. When you plunge wholeheartedly into life, you'll discover that the more you contribute to your world, the more your world will contribute back to you.

So don't settle for a lukewarm existence. Instead, make the character-building choice to become genuinely involved in life. The world needs your enthusiasm . . . and so, by the way, do you.

When we wholeheartedly commit ourselves to God, there is nothing mediocre or run-of-the-mill about us. To live for Christ is to be passionate about our Lord and about our lives.

Jim Gallery

Wherever you are, be all there. Live to the hilt every situation you believe to be the will of God.

Jim Elliot

It is a remarkable thing that some of the most optimistic and enthusiastic people you will meet are those who have been through intense suffering.

Warren Wiersbe

Your enthusiasm will be infectious, stimulating, and attractive to others. They will love you for it. They will go for you and with you.

Norman Vincent Peale

Never be lazy in your work, but serve the Lord enthusiastically.

Romans 12:11 NLT

Character Builder

Don't wait for enthusiasm to find you ... go looking for it.
Look at your life and your relationships as exciting adventures.
Don't wait for life to spice itself; spice things up yourself.

DO IT NOW; BUILD CHARACTER NOW

When you make a vow to God, don't delay fulfilling it, because He does not delight in fools. Fulfill what you vow.

ECCLESIASTES 5:4 HCSB

The habit of putting things off until the last minute, along with its first cousin, the habit of making excuses for work that was never done, can be detrimental to your life and to your character.

Are you in the habit of doing what needs to be done when it needs to be done, or are you a dues-paying member of the Procrastinator's Club? If you've acquired the habit of doing things sooner rather than later, congratulations! But, if you find yourself putting off all those unpleasant tasks until later (or never), it's time to think about the consequences of your behavior.

One way that you can learn to defeat procrastination is by paying less attention to your fears and more attention to your responsibilities. So, when you're faced with a difficult choice or an unpleasant responsibility, don't spend endless hours fretting over your fate. Simply seek God's counsel and get busy. When you do, you will be richly rewarded because of your willingness to act.

Every time you refuse to face up to life and its problems, you weaken your character.

E. Stanley Jones

Action springs not from thought, but from a readiness for responsibility.

Dietrich Bonhoeffer

If doing a good act in public will excite others to do more good, then "Let your Light shine to all." Miss no opportunity to do good.

John Wesley

Now is the only time worth having because, indeed, it is the only time we have.

C. H. Spurgeon

Do noble things, do not dream them all day long.

Charles Kingsley

Character Builder

Today, pick out one important obligation that you've been putting off. Then, take at least one specific step toward the completion of the task you've been avoiding. Even if you don't finish the job, you'll discover that it's easier to finish a job that you've already begun than to finish a job that you've never started.

CONTROLLING THE DIRECTION OF YOUR THOUGHTS

And now, dear brothers and sisters, let me say one more thing as I close this letter. Fix your thoughts on what is true and honorable and right. Think about things that are pure and lovely and admirable. Think about things that are excellent and worthy of praise.

PHILIPPIANS 4:8 NLT

Here's a proven way to build character: learn to control the direction of your thoughts. Your thoughts, of course, are intensely powerful things. Your thoughts have the power to lift you up or drag you down; they have the power to energize you or deplete you, to inspire you to greater accomplishments or to make those accomplishments impossible.

How will you and your family members direct your thoughts today? Will you follow the instructions of Philippians 4:8 by dwelling upon those things that are honorable, true, and worthy of praise? Or will you allow your thoughts to be hijacked by the negativity that seems to dominate our troubled world?

Are you fearful, angry, bored, or worried? Are you so preoccupied with the concerns of this day that you fail to thank God for the promise of eternity? Are you confused, bitter, or pessimistic? If so, God wants to have a little talk with you.

It's up to you and your loved ones to celebrate the life that God has given you by focusing your minds upon "whatever is commendable." So form the habit of spending more time thinking about your blessings and less time fretting about your hardships. Then, take time to thank the Giver of all things good for gifts that are, in truth, far too numerous to count.

The mind is like a clock that is constantly running down. It has to be wound up daily with good thoughts.

FULTON J. SHEEN

God's cure for evil thinking is to fill our minds with that which is good.

GEORGE SWEETING

If our minds are stayed upon God, His peace will rule the affairs entertained by our minds. If, on the other hand, we allow our minds to dwell on the cares of this world, God's peace will be far from our thoughts.

WOODROLL KROLL

CHARACTER BUILDER

Watch what you think. If your inner voice is, in reality, your inner critic, you need to tone down the criticism now. And while you're at it, train yourself to begin thinking thoughts that are more rational, more accepting, and less judgmental.

DAY 33

A WILLINGNESS TO SERVE

You address me as "Teacher" and "Master," and rightly so. That is what I am. So if I, the Master and Teacher, washed your feet, you must now wash each other's feet. I've laid down a pattern for you. What I've done, you do.

JOHN 13:15 MSG

We live in a world that glorifies power, prestige, fame, and money. But the words of Jesus teach us that the most esteemed men and women are not the widely acclaimed leaders of society; the most esteemed among us are the humble servants of society.

Dietrich Bonhoeffer was correct when he observed, "It is very easy to overestimate the importance of our own achievements in comparison with what we owe others." In other words, reality breeds humility . . . and humility should breed service.

Every single day of your life, including this one, God will give you opportunities to serve Him by serving other people. Welcome those opportunities with open arms. Always be willing to pitch in and make the world a better place, and forego the temptation to keep all your blessings to yourself. When you do, you'll earn rewards that are simply unavailable to folks who stubbornly refuse to serve.

Service is a character-building experience: the more you serve, the more you grow. So, as you go about your daily activities, remember this: the Savior of all humanity made Himself a servant . . . and if you want to really know Him better, you must do the same.

In Jesus, the service of God and the service of the least of the brethren were one.

DIETRICH BONHOEFFER

God wants us to serve Him with a willing spirit, one that would choose no other way.

BETH MOORE

Some want to live within the sound of church or chapel bell; I want to run a rescue shop within a yard of hell.

C. T. STUDD

God does not do anything with us, only through us.

OSWALD CHAMBERS

CHARACTER BUILDER

Whatever your age, whatever your circumstances, you can serve: Each stage of life's journey is a glorious opportunity to place yourself in the service of the One who is the Giver of all blessings. As long as you live, you should honor God with your service to others.

OBEDIENCE BUILDS CHARACTER

Not everyone who says to Me, "Lord, Lord!" will enter the kingdom of heaven, but the one who does the will of My Father in heaven.

MATTHEW 7:21 HCSB

Obedience to God is determined, not by words, but by deeds. Talking about character-building is easy; living righteously is far more difficult, especially in today's temptation-filled world.

Since God created Adam and Eve, we human beings have been rebelling against our Creator. Why? Because we are unwilling to trust God's Word, and we are unwilling to follow His instructions. God has given us a guidebook for righteous living called the Holy Bible. It contains thorough guidelines which, if followed, lead to fulfillment, abundance, and salvation. But, if we choose to ignore God's commandments, the results are as predictable as they are unfortunate.

Do you seek God's peace and His blessings? Then obey Him. When you're faced with a difficult choice or a powerful temptation, seek God's counsel and trust the counsel He gives. Invite God into your heart and live according to His commandments. When you do, you will be blessed today, tomorrow, and forever.

Believe and do what God says. The life-changing consequences will be limitless, and the results will be confidence and peace of mind.

FRANKLIN GRAHAM

All true knowledge of God is born out of obedience.

JOHN CALVIN

God is God. Because He is God, He is worthy of my trust and obedience. I will find rest nowhere but in His holy will, a will that is unspeakably beyond my largest notions of what He is up to.

ELISABETH ELLIOT

Obedience that is not motivated by love cannot produce the spiritual fruit that God wants from His children.

WARREN WIERSBE

It is the LORD your God you must follow, and him you must revere. Keep his commands and obey him; serve him and hold fast to him.

DEUTERONOMY 13:4 NIV

CHARACTER BUILDER

Obedience leads to spiritual growth. Oswald Chambers correctly observed, "We grow spiritually as our Lord grew physically: by a life of simple, unobtrusive obedience." When you take these words to heart, you will embark upon a lifetime of spiritual growth ... and God will smile.

THE MEDIA TEARS DOWN CHARACTER

Set your minds on what is above, not on what is on the earth.

COLOSSIANS 3:2 HCSB

Sometimes it's hard to hold on to your integrity, especially when the world keeps pumping out messages that are contrary to your faith and destructive to your character.

The media is working around the clock in an attempt to rearrange your priorities. The media says that your appearance is all-important, that your possessions are all-important, and that "fun" is the ultimate object of life. But guess what? Those messages are lies. The important things in your life have little to do with parties or appearances. The all-important things in life have to do with your faith, your family, and your future. Period.

Are you willing to make the character-building decision to stand up for your faith? If so, you'll be doing yourself a monumental favor. And consider this: When you begin to speak up for God, isn't it logical to assume that you'll also begin to know Him in a more meaningful way? Of course you will.

So forget the media hype, and pay attention to God. Stand up for Him and be counted, not just in church where it's relatively easy to be a Christian, but also outside the church, where it's significantly harder. You owe it God . . . and just as importantly, you owe it to yourself.

As we have by faith said no to sin, so we should by faith say yes to God and set our minds on things above, where Christ is seated in the heavenlies.

Vonette Bright

The more we stuff ourselves with material pleasures, the less we seem to appreciate life.

Barbara Johnson

Our fight is not against any physical enemy; it is against organizations and powers that are spiritual. We must struggle against sin all our lives, but we are assured we will win.

Corrie ten Boom

It is impossible to please God doing things motivated by and produced by the flesh.

Bill Bright

Character Builder

Don't Trust the Media's Messages: Many of the messages that you receive from the media are specifically designed to sell you products that interfere with your spiritual, physical, or emotional health. God takes great interest in your health; the moguls from Madison Avenue take great interest in your pocketbook. Trust God.

BEHAVING DIFFERENTLY

So don't get tired of doing what is good. Don't get discouraged and give up, for we will reap a harvest of blessing at the appropriate time.

If you're like most people, you seek the admiration of your neighbors, your coworkers, and your family members. But the eagerness to please others should never overshadow your eagerness to please God. And your desire to impress others should never cause you to compromise your beliefs or to defy your conscience. In short, you must be a "doer of the word" by putting God first.

The words of Matthew 6:33 offer clear instructions for managing your day and your life: "But seek first the kingdom of God and His righteousness, and all these things will be provided for you" (HCSB).

Each new day presents countless opportunities to put God in first place . . . or not. When you honor Him by living according to His commandments, you earn the abundance and peace that He promises. But, if you ignore God's teachings, you'll pay a price, perhaps a very great price indeed.

Would you like a time-tested formula for successful living? Here it is: Don't just listen to God's Word, live by it. Does this sound too simple? Perhaps it is simple, but it is also the only way to reap the marvelous riches that God has in store for you.

Although God causes all things to work together for good for His children, He still holds us accountable for our behavior.

KAY ARTHUR

Either God's Word keeps you from sin, or sin keeps you from God's Word.

CORRIE TEN BOOM

There may be no trumpet sound or loud applause when we make a right decision, just a calm sense of resolution and peace.

GLORIA GAITHER

The temptation of the age is to look good without being good.

BRENNAN MANNING

If we have the true love of God in our hearts, we will show it in our lives. We will not have to go up and down the earth proclaiming it. We will show it in everything we say or do.

D. L. MOODY

CHARACTER BUILDER

Ask yourself if your behavior has been radically changed by your unfolding relationship with God. If the answer to this question is unclear to you—or if the honest answer is a resounding no—think of a single step you can take, a positive change in your life, that will bring you closer to your Creator.

STAYING OFF THE SLIPPERY SLOPE

Jesus responded, "I assure you: Everyone who commits sin is a slave of sin."

JOHN 8:34 HCSB

The temptations of the world sit atop a slippery slope. If you sample those temptations even once, you're on that slope. Perhaps, if you're lucky, you can keep your footing. Perhaps not. But of this you can be certain: if you never step foot on the slippery slope of sin, you'll never slide off.

You live in a world that encourages you to "try" any number of things which are dangerous to your spiritual, mental, or physical health. It's a world brimming with traps and temptations designed to corrupt your character, ruin your health, sabotage your relationships, and wreck your life. And by the way, you know precisely which temptations are most tempting to you, and therefore the most dangerous.

Invariably, addictive substances and destructive behaviors are described, at least in the beginning, as "harmless" pleasures, but they're not. So your job, as a rational person and a well-meaning Christian, is to do the following: Never experiment with an activity that you wouldn't want to become a full-blown habit. Why? Because when it comes to the temptations of this world, it's easier to stay out than to get out. In other words, the best time to cure a bad habit is before it starts.

Faith in Christ is the victory that overcomes not only the world but also every engrained sin of the flesh.

Jim Cymbala

The heart of man is revealed in temptation. Man knows his sin, which without temptation he could never have known, for it is in temptation man knows on what he has set his heart. The coming to light of sin is the work of the accuser, who thereby thinks to have won the victory. But, it is sin that has become manifest that can be known, and therefore forgiven. Thus, the manifestation of sin belongs to the salvation plan of God with man, and Satan must serve this plan.

Dietrich Bonhoeffer

As a child of God, you are no longer a slave to sin.

Kay Arthur

There is nothing wrong with asking God's direction. But it is wrong to go our own way, then expect Him to bail us out.

Larry Burkett

Character Builder

When given the opportunity to "try" something that might turn into a bad habit, don't. The slippery slope might be steeper than it looks.

GENEROSITY BUILDS CHARACTER

Freely you have received, freely give.

MATTHEW 10:8 NIV

Every time you give generously to those who need your help, you're strengthening your character. So, if you're looking for a surefire way to improve the quality of your life, here it is: be more generous.

The thread of generosity is woven—completely and inextricably—into the very fabric of Christ's teachings. As He sent His disciples out to heal the sick and spread God's message of salvation, Jesus offered this guiding principle: "Freely you have received, freely give" (Matthew 10:8 NIV). The principle still applies. If we are to be disciples of Christ, we must give freely of our time, our possessions, and our love.

In 2 Corinthians 9, Paul reminds us that when we sow the seeds of generosity, we reap bountiful rewards in accordance with God's plan for our lives. Thus, we are instructed to give cheerfully and without reservation: "But this I say: He who sows sparingly will also reap sparingly, and he who sows bountifully will also reap bountifully. So let each one give as he purposes in his heart, not grudgingly or of necessity; for God loves a cheerful giver" (vv. 6-7 NKJV).

Today, you may feel the urge to hoard your blessings. Don't do it. Instead, give generously to those less fortunate than you. Find a need and fill it. Lend a helping hand and share a word of kindness. It's the godly thing to do—and it's the best way to live.

Nothing is really ours until we share it.

C. S. Lewis

The measure of a life, after all, is not its duration but its donation.

Corrie ten Boom

We can't do everything, but can we do anything more valuable than invest ourselves in another?

Elisabeth Elliot

Generosity is changing one's focus from self to others.

John Maxwell

God has given gifts to each of you from his great variety of spiritual gifts. Manage them well so that God's generosity can flow through you.

1 Peter 4:10 NLT

Character Builder

Would you like to be a little happier? Try sharing a few more of the blessings that God has bestowed upon you. In other words, if you want to be happy, be generous. And if you want to be unhappy, be greedy. And if you're not sure about the best way to give, pray about it.

DAY 39

BEYOND DISCOURAGEMENT

But as for you, be strong; don't be discouraged, for your work has a reward.

2 CHRONICLES 15:7 HCSB

We Christians have many reasons to celebrate. Yet sometimes, even the most devout men and women may become discouraged. After all, we live in a world where expectations can be high and demands can be even higher. When we fail to meet the expectations of others (or, for that matter, the expectations that we have set for ourselves), we may be tempted to abandon hope. But God has other plans. He knows exactly how He intends to use us. Our task is to remain faithful until He does.

When we are discouraged—on those cloudy days when our strength is sapped and our faith is shaken—there exists a source from which we can draw courage and wisdom. That source is God. When we seek to form a more intimate and dynamic relationship with our Creator, He renews our spirits and restores our souls. This promise is made clear in Isaiah 40:

"Have you not known? Have you not heard? The everlasting God, the Lord, the Creator of the ends of the earth, neither faints nor is weary. His understanding is unsearchable. He gives power to the weak, and to those who have no might He increases strength. Even the youths shall faint and be weary, and the young men shall utterly fall,

but those who wait on the Lord shall renew their strength; they shall mount up with wings like eagles, they shall run and not be weary, they shall walk and not faint." (vv. 28-31 NKJV)

God offers us the strength to meet our challenges, and He offers us hope for the future. So, if you have become discouraged with the direction of your day or your life, turn your thoughts and prayers to God—and associate with like-minded believers who do the same. And remember this: your Heavenly Father is a God of possibility, not negativity. He is your Shepherd; He never leaves your side; and the ultimate victory will be His. So how, then, can you ever stay discouraged for long?

God does not dispense strength and encouragement like a druggist fills your prescription. The Lord doesn't promise to give us something to take so we can handle our weary moments. He promises us Himself. That is all. And that is enough.

Charles Swindoll

Overcoming discouragement is simply a matter of taking away the DIS and adding the EN.

Barbara Johnson

Character Builder

If you're feeling discouraged, try to redirect your thoughts away from the troubles that plague you—focus, instead, upon the opportunities that surround you.

SPIRITUAL WARFARE

Therefore, submit to God. But resist the Devil, and he will flee from you. Draw near to God, and He will draw near to you. Cleanse your hands, sinners, and purify your hearts, double-minded people!

JAMES 4:7-8 HCSB

You live in a world where it can be tough to maintain your integrity. Temptations are everywhere, and the devil, it seems, never takes a day off. Your challenge is to see those temptations for what they are: dangerous and destructive.

In his letter to Jewish Christians, Peter offered a stern warning: "Your adversary, the devil, prowls around like a roaring lion, seeking someone to devour" (1 Peter 5:8 NASB). What was true in New Testament times is equally true in our own. Evil is indeed abroad in the world, and Satan continues to sow the seeds of destruction far and wide. In a very real sense, our world is at war: good versus evil, addiction versus moderation, hope versus suffering, praise versus apathy. As Christians, we must ensure that we place ourselves squarely on the right side of these conflicts: God's side. How can we do it? By thoughtfully studying God's Word, by regularly worshiping with fellow believers, and by guarding our hearts and minds against the subtle temptations of the enemy. When we do, we are protected.

There is nothing evil in matter itself. Evil lies in the spirit. Evils of the heart, of the mind, of the soul, of the spirit—these have to do with man's sin, and the only reason the human body does evil is because the human spirit uses it to do evil.

A. W. Tozer

Light is stronger than darkness—darkness cannot "comprehend" or "overcome" it.

Anne Graham Lotz

The only thing necessary for the triumph of evil is for good men to do nothing.

Edmund Burke

Rebuke the Enemy in your own name and he laughs; command him in the name of Christ and he flees.

John Eldredge

CHARACTER BUILDER

It's out there, and it can hurt you. Evil does exist, and you will confront it. Prepare yourself by forming a genuine, life-changing relationship with God and His only begotten Son. There is darkness in this world, but God's light can overpower any darkness.

83

STRONG MENTORS HELP BUILD CHARACTER

Listen to advice and accept correction, and in the end you will be wise.

PROVERBS 19:20 NCV

Would you like a surefire way to build character? If so, then you should find suitable mentors—men and women whose character you admire—and imitate them.

A savvy mentor can help you make character-building choices. And just as importantly, a thoughtful mentor can help you recognize and avoid the hidden big-time mistakes that can derail your day (or your life).

Wise mentors aren't really very hard to find if you look in the right places (but they're almost impossible to find if you look in the wrong places!). So today, as an exercise in character-building, select from your friends and family members a mentor whose judgment you trust. Then listen carefully to your mentor's advice and be willing to accept that advice even if accepting it requires effort or pain, or both. Consider your mentor to be God's gift to you. Thank God for that gift, and use it.

The next best thing to being wise oneself is to live in a circle of those who are.

C. S. Lewis

It takes a wise person to give good advice, but an even wiser person to take it.

Marie T. Freeman

The man who never reads will never be read; he who never quotes will never be quoted. He who will not use the thoughts of other men's brains proves that he has no brains of his own.

C. H. Spurgeon

The effective mentor strives to help a man or woman discover what they can be in Christ and then holds them accountable to become that person.

Howard Hendricks

Character Builder

Rely on the advice of trusted friends and mentors.
Proverbs 1:5 makes it clear: "A wise man will hear and increase
learning, and a man of understanding will attain wise counsel"
(NKJV). Do you want to be wise?
Seek counsel from wise people, starting today.

DAY 42

YOU'RE ACCOUNTABLE

But each person should examine his own work, and then he will have a reason for boasting in himself alone, and not in respect to someone else. For each person will have to carry his own load.

GALATIANS 6:4-5 HCSB

We humans are masters at passing the buck. Why? Because passing the buck is easier than fixing, and criticizing others is so much easier than improving ourselves. So instead of solving our problems legitimately (by doing the work required to solve them), we are inclined to fret, to blame, and to criticize, while doing precious little else. When we do, our problems, quite predictably, remain unsolved.

Whether you like it or not, you (and only you) are accountable for your actions. But because you are human, you'll be sorely tempted to pass the blame. Avoid that temptation at all costs.

Problem-solving builds character. Every time you straighten your back and look squarely into the face of Old Man Trouble, you'll strengthen not only your backbone but also your spirit. So, instead of looking for someone to blame, look for something to fix, and then get busy fixing it. And as you consider your own situation, remember this: God has a way of helping those who help themselves, but He doesn't spend much time helping those who don't.

Generally speaking, accountability is a willingness to share our activities, conduct, and fulfillment of assigned responsibilities with others.

Charles Stanley

Though I know intellectually how vulnerable I am to pride and power, I am the last one to know when I succumb to their seduction. That's why spiritual Lone Rangers are so dangerous—and why we must depend on trusted brothers and sisters who love us enough to tell us the truth.

Chuck Colson

We urgently need people who encourage and inspire us to move toward God and away from the world's enticing pleasures.

Jim Cymbala

What difference does it make to you what someone else becomes, or says, or does? You do not need to answer for others, only for yourself.

Thomas à Kempis

Character Builder

It's easy to hold other people accountable, but real accountability begins with the person in the mirror. Think about one specific area of responsibility that is uniquely yours, and think about a specific step you can take today to better fulfill that responsibility.

SLOTH DESTROYS CHARACTER

But one thing I do: Forgetting what is behind and straining toward what is ahead, I press on toward the goal to win the prize for which God has called me heavenward in Christ Jesus.

PHILIPPIANS 3:13-14 NIV

I f you'd like a surefire formula for tearing down your character, here it is: do everything you can to avoid doing an honest day's work. But if you'd like a proven formula for building character, do your work with vigor, dedication, and enthusiasm.

You've heard the advice since you were a child: "Give the boss an honest day's work for an honest day's pay." But sometimes, you'll be tempted to do otherwise. Why? For starters, no job is perfect—and that means that your job isn't perfect, either. So, from time to time, you'll probably become upset with your job, and it is during these times, when you're frustrated or upset, that you'll be tempted to gripe, to waste time, and to do little else. Avoid these temptations—they're self-destructive.

Even if you're planning on quitting your job tomorrow, give your boss a full day's work today. Otherwise, you'll be developing a very bad habit: the habit of giving less than 100%. It's a character-destroying trait, an easy habit to acquire and a difficult habit to break.

If you're looking for folks to waste time with, you can probably find them just about anywhere—including your workplace. But if you're looking for a meaningful life (not to mention a career that you love), make up your mind to be the kind of person whose work speaks (in glowing terms) for itself. When you do, you'll discover that when you give your best, you enjoy work the most.

The worst thing that laziness does is rob a man of spiritual purpose.

BILLY GRAHAM

The only cure for laziness is to be filled with the life of God.

OSWALD CHAMBERS

Idleness and pride tax with a heavier hand than kings and governments.

BEN FRANKLIN

Work is such a beautiful and helpful thing, and independence so delightful that I wonder why there are any lazy people in the world.

LOUISA MAY ALCOTT

CHARACTER BUILDER

Feeling a little lazy? That means that you're not excited about your work. So here's your challenge: find work that's so much fun you can't wait to clock in. When you do, you'll discover that a really good job beats leisure (or retirement) hands down.

TRUSTING HIS PROMISES

Let us hold on to the confession of our hope without wavering, for He who promised is faithful.

HEBREWS 10:23 HCSB

When you trust God's promises—and when you try your best to honor Him with your prayers, your thoughts, and your actions—you will continue building character every day of your life.

Are you willing to trust God completely, or are you living beneath a cloud of doubt and fear? God's Word makes it clear: you should trust Him and His promises; when you do, you will live wisely and well.

Are you tired? Discouraged? Fearful? Be comforted and trust the promises that God has made to you. Are you struggling against a powerful temptation? Be courageous and call upon God. He will give you the strength to rise above your challenges. Are you confused? Listen to the quiet voice of your Heavenly Father. He is not a God of confusion. Talk with Him; listen to Him; trust Him, and trust His promises. He is steadfast, and He is your Protector . . . forever.

There are four words I wish we would never forget, and they are, "God keeps his word."

CHARLES SWINDOLL

The stars may fall, but God's promises will stand and be fulfilled.

J. I. PACKER

We honor God by asking for great things when they are a part of His promise. We dishonor Him and cheat ourselves when we ask for molehills where He has promised mountains.

VANCE HAVNER

The promises of Scripture are not mere pious hopes or sanctified guesses. They are more than sentimental words to be printed on decorated cards for Sunday School children. They are eternal verities. They are true. There is no perhaps about them.

PETER MARSHALL

Patient endurance is what you need now, so you will continue to do God's will. Then you will receive all that he has promised.

HEBREWS 10:36 NLT

CHARACTER BUILDER

Do you really trust God's promises, or are you hedging your bets? Today, think about the role that God's Word plays in your life, and think about ways that you can worry less and trust God more.

REAL TRANSFORMATION? INNER TRANSFORMATION!

Therefore if anyone is in Christ, he is a new creature; the old things passed away; behold, new things have come.

2 CORINTHIANS 5:17 HCSB

Have you invited God's Son to reign over your heart and your life? If so, think for a moment about the "old" you, the person you were before you invited Christ into your heart. Now, think about the "new" you, the person you have become since then. Is there a difference between the "old" you and the "new and improved" version? There should be! And that difference should be noticeable not only to you but also to others.

Warren Wiersbe observed, "The greatest miracle of all is the transformation of a lost sinner into a child of God." And Oswald Chambers noted, "If the Spirit of God has transformed you within, you will exhibit Divine characteristics in your life, not good human characteristics. God's life in us expresses itself as God's life, not as a human life trying to be godly."

When you invited Christ to reign over your heart, you became a new creation through Him. This day offers yet another opportunity to behave yourself like that new creation by serving your Creator and strengthening your character. When you do, God will guide your steps and bless your endeavors today and forever.

No man is ever the same after God has laid His hand upon him.

A. W. Tozer

Being born again is God's solution to our need for love and life and light.

Anne Graham Lotz

The transforming love of God has repositioned me for eternity. I am now a new man, forgiven, basking in the warm love of our living God, trusting His promises and provision, and enjoying life to the fullest.

Bill Bright

What is God looking for? He is looking for men and women whose hearts are completely His.

Charles Swindoll

When I met Christ, I felt that I had swallowed sunshine.

E. Stanley Jones

Character Builder

Today, remember this: a true conversion experience results in a life transformed by Christ and a commitment to following in His footsteps.

MATERIALISM TEARS DOWN CHARACTER

Don't collect for yourselves treasures on earth, where moth and rust destroy and where thieves break in and steal. But collect for yourselves treasures in heaven, where neither moth nor rust destroys, and where thieves don't break in and steal. For where your treasure is, there your heart will be also.

MATTHEW 6:19-21 HCSB

In our modern society, we need money to live, but we should never make the acquisition of money the central focus of our lives. Money is a tool, but it should never overwhelm our sensibilities. The focus of life must be squarely on things spiritual, not things material.

Whenever we become absorbed with the acquisition of things, complications arise. Each new acquisition costs money or time, often both. To further complicate matters, many items can be purchased, not with real money, but with something much more insidious: debt. Debt—especially consumer debt used to purchase depreciating assets—is a modern-day form of indentured servitude.

If you're looking for a sure-fire, time-tested way to simplify your life and thereby improve your world, learn to control your possessions before they control you. Purchase only those things that make a significant contribution to your well-being and the well-being of your family. Never spend more than you make.

Understand the folly in buying consumer goods on credit. Never use credit cards as a way of financing your lifestyle.

Ask yourself this simple question: "Do I own my possessions, or do they own me?" If you don't like the answer you receive, make an iron-clad promise to stop acquiring and start divesting. As you simplify your life, you'll be amazed at the things you can do without. You'll be pleasantly surprised at the sense of satisfaction that accompanies your new-found moderation. And you'll understand first-hand that when it comes to material possessions, less truly is more.

So, if you find yourself wrapped up in the concerns of the material world, it's time to reorder your priorities by turning your thoughts and your prayers to more important matters. And, it's time to begin storing up riches that will endure throughout eternity: the spiritual kind.

When possessions become our god, we become materialistic and greedy . . . and we forfeit our contentment and our joy.

CHARLES SWINDOLL

CHARACTER BUILDER

Materialism Made Simple: The world wants you to believe that "money and stuff" can buy happiness. Don't believe it! Genuine happiness comes not from money, but from the things that money can't buy—starting, of course, with your relationship to God and His only begotten Son.

NEED SOMETHING FROM GOD? ASK!

You do not have, because you do not ask God.

JAMES 4:2 NIV

How often do you ask God for His help and His wisdom? Occasionally? Intermittently? Whenever you experience a crisis? Hopefully not. Hopefully, you've acquired the habit of asking for God's assistance early and often. And hopefully, you have learned to seek His guidance in every aspect of your life.

Jesus made it clear to His disciples: they should petition God to meet their needs. So should you. Genuine, heartfelt prayer produces powerful changes in you and in your world. When you lift your heart to God, you open yourself to a never-ending source of divine wisdom and infinite love.

James 5:16 makes a promise that God intends to keep: when you pray earnestly, fervently, and often, great things will happen. Too many people are too timid or too pessimistic to ask God to do big things. Please don't count yourself among their number.

God can do great things through you if you have the courage to ask Him (and the determination to keep asking Him). But don't expect Him to do all the work. When you do your part, He will do His part—and when He does, you can expect miracles to happen.

The Bible promises that God will guide you if you let Him. Your job is to let Him. But sometimes, you will be tempted to do otherwise. Sometimes, you'll be tempted to go along with the crowd; other times, you'll be tempted to do things your way, not God's way. When you feel those temptations, resist them.

God has promised that when you ask for His help, He will not withhold it. So ask. Ask Him to meet the needs of your day. Ask Him to lead you, to protect you, and to correct you. Then, trust the answers He gives.

God stands at the door and waits. When you knock, He opens. When you ask, He answers. Your task, of course, to make God a full partner in every aspect of your life—and to seek His guidance prayerfully, confidently, and often.

We honor God by asking for great things when they are a part of His promise. We dishonor Him and cheat ourselves when we ask for molehills where He has promised mountains.

VANCE HAVNER

We get into trouble when we think we know what to do and we stop asking God if we're doing it.

STORMIE OMARTIAN

CHARACTER BUILDER

Today, think of a specific need that is weighing heavily on your heart. Then, spend a few quiet moments asking God for His guidance and for His help.

USING THE TALENTS HE GAVE YOU

I remind you to keep ablaze the gift of God that is in you.

2 TIMOTHY 1:6 HCSB

C haracter-development and talent-development often go hand-in-hand. All of us have special talents, and you are no exception. But your talent is no guarantee of success; it must be cultivated and nurtured; otherwise, it will go unused . . . and God's gift to you will be squandered.

In the 25th chapter of Matthew, Jesus tells the "Parable of the Talents." In it, He describes a master who leaves his servants with varying amounts of money (talents). When the master returns, some servants have put their money to work and earned more, to which the master responds, "Well done, good and faithful servant! You have been faithful with a few things; I will put you in charge of many things. Come and share your master's happiness!" (Matthew 25:21 NIV)

But the story does not end so happily for the foolish servant who was given a single talent but did nothing with it. For this man, the master has nothing but reproach: "You wicked, lazy servant...." (Matthew 25:26 NIV) The message from Jesus is clear: We must use our talents, not waste them.

Your particular talent is a treasure on temporary loan from God. He intends that your talent enrich the world and enrich your life. Value the gift that God has given you, nourish it, make it grow, and share it with the world. Then, when you meet your Master face-to-face, you, too, will hear those wonderful words, "Well done, good and faithful servant! . . . Come and share your Master's happiness!"

God often reveals His direction for our lives through the way He made us . . . with a certain personality and unique skills.

Bill Hybels

You are the only person on earth who can use your ability.

Zig Ziglar

God has given gifts to each of you from his great variety of spiritual gifts. Manage them well so that God's generosity can flow through you.

1 Peter 4:10 NLT

Character Builder

Converting raw talent into polished skill usually requires work, and lots of it. God's Word clearly instructs you to do the hard work of refining your talents for the glory of His kingdom and the service of His people. So, we are wise to remember the old adage: "What you are is God's gift to you; what you become is your gift to God." And it's up to you to make sure that your gift is worthy of the Giver.

DAY 49

VALUE-BASED DECISIONS

Walk in a manner worthy of the God who calls you into His own kingdom and glory.

1 THESSALONIANS 2:12 NASB

Whether you realize it or not, your character is shaped by your values. From the time your alarm clock wakes you up in the morning until the moment you lay your head on the pillow at night, your actions are guided by the values that you hold most dear. If you're a thoughtful believer, then those values are shaped by the Word of God.

Society seeks to impose its set of values upon you, however these values are often contrary to God's Word (and thus contrary to your own best interests). The world makes promises that it simply cannot fulfill. It promises happiness, contentment, prosperity, and abundance. But genuine abundance is not a by-product of possessions or status; it is a by-product of your thoughts, your actions, and your relationship with God. The world's promises are incomplete and deceptive; God's promises are unfailing. Your challenge, then, is to build your value system upon the firm foundation of God's promises . . . nothing else will suffice.

As a citizen of the 21st century, you live in a world that is filled with countless opportunities to make big-time mistakes. The world seems to cry, "Worship me with your time, your money, your energy, and your thoughts!" But God commands otherwise: He instructs you to worship Him and Him alone; everything else must be secondary.

Do you want to strengthen your character? If so, then you must build your life upon a value system that puts God first. So, when you're faced with a difficult choice or a powerful temptation, seek God's counsel and trust the counsel that He gives. Invite God into your heart and live according to His commandments. Study His Word and talk to Him often. When you do, you will share in the abundance and peace that only God can give.

We can be secure in the knowledge that our value and worth are not dependent upon who we are or what we think or say or do. It is based on who we are in Christ Jesus.

JOYCE MEYER

As the first community to which a person is attached and the first authority under which a person learns to live, the family establishes society's most basic values.

CHARLES COLSON

CHARACTER BUILDER

Whose values will you share? You can have the values that the world holds dear, or you can have the values that God holds dear, but you can't have both. The decision is yours ... and so are the consequences.

STRONG ENOUGH TO ENCOURAGE OTHERS

Let's see how inventive we can be in encouraging love and helping out, not avoiding worshipping together as some do but spurring each other on.

HEBREWS 10:24-25 MSG

Want to build character and, at the same time, build a better life? Then find thoughtful, honorable, God-fearing people who will offer you a steady stream of encouragement.

Life is a team sport, and all of us need occasional pats on the back from our teammates. As Christians, we are called upon to spread the Good News of Christ, and we are also called to spread a message of encouragement and hope to the world.

In the book of Ephesians, Paul writes, "Do not let any unwholesome talk come out of your mouths, but only what is helpful for building others up according to their needs, that it may benefit those who listen" (4:29 NIV). Paul reminds us that when we choose our words carefully, we can have a powerful impact on those around us.

Whether you realize it or not, many people with whom you come in contact every day are in desperate need of a smile or an encouraging word. The world can be a difficult place, and countless friends and family members may be troubled by the challenges of everyday life. Since we don't always know who needs our help, the best strategy is to encourage all the people who cross our paths. So today, be a world-class source of encouragement to everyone you meet. Never has the need been greater.

The secret of success is to find a need and fill it, to find a hurt and heal it, to find somebody with a problem and offer to help solve it.

Robert Schuller

Do you wonder where you can go for encouragement and motivation? Run to Jesus.

Max Lucado

I want their hearts to be encouraged and joined together in love, so that they may have all the riches of assured understanding, and have the knowledge of God's mystery—Christ.

Colossians 2:2 HCSB

Character Builder

Do you want to be successful? Encourage others to do the same.
You can't lift other people up without lifting yourself up, too.
And remember the words of Oswald Chambers:
"God grant that we may not hinder those who are battling their way slowly into the light."

BEYOND EXCUSES

Let us live in a right way . . . clothe yourselves with the Lord Jesus Christ and forget about satisfying your sinful self.

ROMANS 13:13-14 NCV

Excuses and character-building don't mix. If you want to build character—and if you want to keep building it—you'll need to avoid the unseemly habit of excuse-making. No exceptions.

We live in a world where excuses are everywhere. And it's precisely because excuses are so numerous that they are also so ineffective. When we hear the words, "I'm sorry but . . .", most of us know exactly what is to follow: The Big Excuse. The dog ate the homework. Traffic was terrible. It's the company's fault. The boss is to blame. The equipment is broken. We're out of that. And so forth, and so on.

Because we humans are such creative excuse-makers, all of the really good excuses have already been taken. In fact, the high-quality excuses have been used, re-used, over-used, and a-bused. That's why excuses don't work—we've heard them all before.

So, if you're wasting your time trying to portray yourself as a victim (and weakening your character in the process), or if you're trying to concoct a new and improved excuse, don't bother. Excuses don't work, and while you're inventing them, neither do you.

Replace your excuses with fresh determination.

CHARLES SWINDOLL

We need to stop focusing on our lacks and stop giving out excuses and start looking at and listening to Jesus.

ANNE GRAHAM LOTZ

An excuse is only the skin of a reason stuffed with a lie.

VANCE HAVNER

Making up a string of excuses is usually harder than doing the work.

MARIE T. FREEMAN

In a crisis, don't hide behind anything or anybody. They're going to find you anyway.

BEAR BRYANT

CHARACTER BUILDER

Today, think of something important that you've been putting off.
Then think of the excuses you've used to avoid that responsibility.
Finally, ask yourself what you can do today to finish
the work you've been avoiding.

Beyond Worry

So do not worry, saying, "What shall we eat?" or "What shall we drink?" or "What shall we wear?" For the pagans run after all these things, and your Heavenly Father knows that you need them. But seek first his kingdom and his righteousness, and all these things will be given to you as well. Therefore do not worry about tomorrow, for tomorrow will worry about itself. Each day has enough trouble of its own.

MATTHEW 6:31-34 NIV

I t's hard to build character when we're worrying about everything in sight. But because life is sometimes difficult, and because we have understandable fears about the uncertainty of the future, we still manage to fret over the countless details of everyday life. We may worry about our relationships, our finances, our health, our habits, or any number of potential problems, some large and some small.

If you're a "worrier" by nature, it's probably time to rethink the way that you think! Perhaps you've formed the unfortunate habit of focusing too intently on negative aspects of life while spending too little time counting your blessings. If so, take your worries to God . . . and leave them there. When you do, you'll learn to worry a little less and to trust God a little more—and that's as it should be because God is trustworthy, you are protected, and your future can be intensely bright.

Much that worries us beforehand can, quite unexpectedly, have a happy and simple solution. Worries just don't matter. Things really are in a better hand than ours.

DIETRICH BONHOEFFER

Today is mine. Tomorrow is none of my business. If I peer anxiously into the fog of the future, I will strain my spiritual eyes so that I will not see clearly what is required of me now.

ELISABETH ELLIOTT

The beginning of anxiety is the end of faith, and the beginning of true faith is the end of anxiety.

GEORGE MUELLER

Bathe each day in prayer! Trying to carry the weight of tomorrow with today's grace will clip your wings and keep you from soaring.

ANNIE CHAPMAN

Let not your heart be troubled; you believe in God, believe also in Me.

JOHN 14:1 NKJV

CHARACTER BUILDER

Assiduously divide your areas of concern into two categories: those you can control and those you cannot. Resolve never to waste time or energy worrying about the latter.

Too Many Distractions?

Let us lay aside every weight and the sin that so easily ensnares us, and run with endurance the race that lies before us, keeping our eyes on Jesus, the source and perfecter of our faith.

Hebrews 12:1-2 HCSB

All of us must live through those days when the traffic jams, the computer crashes, and the dog makes a main course out of our homework. But, when we find ourselves distracted by the minor frustrations of life, we must catch ourselves, take a deep breath, and lift our thoughts upward.

Although we must sometimes struggle mightily to rise above the distractions of everyday living, we need never struggle alone. God is here—eternal and faithful, with infinite patience and love—and, if we reach out to Him, He will restore our sense of perspective and give peace to our hearts.

Today, as an exercise in character-building, make this promise to yourself and keep it: promise to focus your thoughts on things that are really important, things like your faith, your family, your friends, and your future. Don't allow the day's interruptions to derail your most important work. And don't allow other people (or the media) to decide what's important to you and your family.

Distractions are everywhere, but, thankfully, so is God . . . and that fact has everything to do with how you prioritize your day and your life.

Setting goals is one way you can be sure that you will focus your efforts on the main things so that trivial matters will not become your focus.

CHARLES STANLEY

When Jesus is in our midst, He brings His limitless power along as well. But, Jesus must be in the middle, all eyes and hearts focused on Him.

SHIRLEY DOBSON

We need to stop focusing on our lacks and stop giving out excuses and start looking at and listening to Jesus.

ANNE GRAHAM LOTZ

Among the enemies to devotion, none is so harmful as distractions. Whatever excites the curiosity, scatters the thoughts, disquiets the heart, absorbs the interests, or shifts our life focus from the kingdom of God within us to the world around us—that is a distraction; and the world is full of them.

A. W. TOZER

CHARACTER BUILDER

Take a few minutes to consider the everyday distractions that are interfering with your life and your faith. Then, jot down at least three ideas for minimizing those distractions or eliminating them altogether.

YOUR CHARACTER, YOUR FAMILY

Choose for yourselves today the one you will worship . . . . As for me and my family, we will worship the Lord.

JOSHUA 24:15 HCSB

A loving family is a treasure from God. If God has blessed you with a close knit, supportive clan, offer a word of thanks to your Creator because He has given you one of His most precious earthly possessions. Your obligation, in response to God's gift, is to treat your family in ways that are consistent with His commandments.

You live in a fast-paced, demanding world, a place where life can be difficult and pressures can be intense. As those pressures build, you may tend to focus so intently upon your obligations that you lose sight, albeit temporarily, of your spiritual and emotional needs (that's one reason why a regular daily devotional time is so important; it offers a badly-needed dose of perspective).

Even when the demands of everyday life are great, you must never forget that you have been entrusted with a profound responsibility: the responsibility of contributing to your family's emotional and spiritual well-being. It's a big job, but with God's help, you're up to the task.

When you place God squarely in the center of your family's life—when you worship Him, praise Him, trust Him, and love Him—then He will most certainly bless you and yours in ways that you could have scarcely imagined.

So the next time your family life becomes a little stressful, remember this: That little band of men, women, kids, and babies is a priceless treasure on temporary loan from the Father above. And it's your responsibility to praise God for that gift—and to act accordingly.

When you think about it for a moment, it certainly makes sense that if people can establish a loving and compatible relationship at home, they have a better chance of establishing winning relationships with those with whom they work on a regular basis.

ZIG ZIGLAR

You cannot honor your family without nurturing you own sense of personal value and honor.

STEPHEN COVEY

Living life with a consistent spiritual walk deeply influences those we love most.

VONETTE BRIGHT

CHARACTER BUILDER

Today, think about the importance of saying "yes" to your family even if it means saying "no" to other obligations.

TAKING TIME TO PRAISE GOD

I will praise you, Lord, with all my heart. I will tell all the miracles you have done. I will be happy because of you; God Most High, I will sing praises to your name.

PSALM 9:1-2 NCV

If you'd like to strengthen your character, try spending more time praising God. And when, by the way, is the best time to praise God? In church? Before dinner is served? When we tuck little children into bed? None of the above. The best time to praise God is all day, every day, to the greatest extent we can, with thanksgiving in our hearts.

Too many of us, even well-intentioned believers, tend to "compartmentalize" our waking hours into a few familiar categories: work, rest, play, family time, and worship. To do so is a mistake. Worship and praise should be woven into the fabric of everything we do; it should never be relegated to a weekly three-hour visit to church on Sunday morning.

Hymn writer James Montgomery advised, "Stand up and bless the Lord, ye people of his choice; stand up and bless the Lord your God with heart and soul and voice." So today, find a little more time to lift your concerns to God in prayer and praise Him for all that He has done. He's listening . . . and He wants to hear from you.

Be not afraid of saying too much in the praises of God; all the danger is of saying too little.

MATTHEW HENRY

When we come before the Lord with praise, humbly repent of our transgressions, and in obedience present our petitions to God according to the guidelines set out for us in Scripture, He will answer.

SHIRLEY DOBSON

Praise opens the window of our hearts, preparing us to walk more closely with God. Prayer raises the window of our spirit, enabling us to listen more clearly to the Father.

MAX LUCADO

Two wings are necessary to lift our souls toward God: prayer and praise. Prayer asks. Praise accepts the answer.

MRS. CHARLES E. COWMAN

CHARACTER BUILDER

Remember that it always pays to praise your Creator.
That's why thoughtful believers (like you) make it a habit to
carve out quiet moments throughout the day to praise God.

BUILDING CHARACTER BY FINDING COURAGE

Be strong and courageous, and do the work. Do not be afraid or discouraged, for the Lord God, my God, is with you.

1 CHRONICLES 28:20 NIV

Courage builds character and vice versa. So if you'd like a brief course in character-building, try this: the next time you face a choice between doing the right thing or the easy thing, summon the courage to do the right thing. And while you're summoning that courage, ask God to help.

Billy Graham observed, "Down through the centuries, in times of trouble and trial, God has brought courage to the hearts of those who love Him. The Bible is filled with assurances of God's help and comfort in every kind of trouble which might cause fears to arise in the human heart. You can look ahead with promise, hope, and joy." Dr. Graham's words apply to you.

The next time you find your courage tested by the inevitable challenges of life, remember that God is as near as your next breath. He is your shield and your strength; He is your protector and your deliverer. Call upon Him in your hour of need and then be comforted. Whatever your challenge, whatever your trouble, God can handle it. And will.

Take courage. We walk in the wilderness today and in the Promised Land tomorrow.

D. L. Moody

What is courage? It is the ability to be strong in trust, in conviction, in obedience. To be courageous is to step out in faith—to trust and obey, no matter what.

Kay Arthur

If a person fears God, he or she has no reason to fear anything else. On the other hand, if a person does not fear God, then fear becomes a way of life.

Beth Moore

When once we are assured that God is good, then there can be nothing left to fear.

Hannah Whitall Smith

Character Builder

Is your courage being tested today? Cling tightly to God's promises, and pray. God can give you the strength to meet any challenge, and that's exactly what you should ask Him to do.

DAY 57

SEEKING GOD'S PLANS

"For I know the plans I have for you"—[this is] the Lord's declaration—"plans for [your] welfare, not for disaster, to give you a future and a hope."

"Why did God put me here?" It's a simple question to ask and, at times, a very complicated question to answer.

As you seek to discover (or perhaps, to rediscover) God's plan for your life, you should start by remembering this: You are here because God put you here, and He did so for a very good reason: His reason.

At times, you may be confident that you are doing God's will. But on other occasions, you may be uncertain about the direction that your life should take. At times, you may wander aimlessly in a wilderness of your own making. And sometimes, you may struggle mightily against God in a vain effort to find success and happiness through your own means, not His. But wherever you find yourself—whether on the mountaintops, in the valleys, or at the crossroads of life—you may be assured that God is there . . . and you may be assured that He has a plan.

If you manage to align yourself with God's plan for your life, you will be energized, you will be enthused, and you will be blessed. That's why you should strive mightily to understand what it is that God wants you to do. But how can you know precisely what God's intentions are? The answer, of course, is that even the most well-intentioned believers face periods of uncertainty and doubt about the direction of their lives. So, too, will you.

When you arrive at one of life's inevitable crossroads, that's the moment when you should turn your thoughts and prayers toward God. When you do, He will make Himself known to you in a time and manner of His choosing. When you discover God's plan for your life, you will experience abundance, peace, joy, and power—God's power.

And that's the only kind of power that really matters.

One of the wonderful things about being a Christian is the knowledge that God has a plan for our lives.

WARREN WIERSBE

If God declares what it means to be human, then our lives are not the meaningless collections of unrelated events they so often appear to be.

STANLEY GRENZ

CHARACTER BUILDER

God has a wonderful plan for your life. And the time to start looking for that plan—and living it—is now. And remember—discovering God's plan begins with prayer, but it doesn't end there. You've also got to work at it.

MONEY:
TOOL OR MASTER?

For the love of money is a root of all sorts of evil, and some by longing for it have wandered away from the faith and pierced themselves with many griefs.

1 TIMOTHY 6:10 NASB

Here's a scary thought: the content of your character is demonstrated by the way you choose to spend money. If you spend money wisely, and if you give God His fair share, then you're doing just fine. But if you're up to your eyeballs in debt, and if "shop till you drop" is your unofficial motto, it's time to retire the credit cards and rearrange your priorities.

Our society is in love with money and the things that money can buy. God is not. God cares about people, not possessions, and so must we. We must, to the best of our abilities, love our neighbors as ourselves, and we must, to the best of our abilities, resist the mighty temptation to place possessions ahead of people.

Money, in and of itself, is not evil; worshipping money is. So today, as you prioritize matters of importance for you and yours, remember that God is almighty, but the dollar is not.

Are you choosing to make money your master? If so, it's time to turn your thoughts and your prayers to more important matters. And, it's time to begin storing up riches that will endure throughout eternity: the spiritual kind.

Servants of God are always more concerned about ministry than money.

RICK WARREN

No man can stand in front of Jesus Christ and say "I want to make money."

OSWALD CHAMBERS

Money separates people more often than it joins them.

LIZ CURTIS HIGGS

There is no correlation between wealth and happiness.

LARRY BURKETT

The borrower is a slave to the lender.

PROVERBS 22:7 HCSB

CHARACTER BUILDER

Put God where He belongs—first: Any relationship that doesn't honor God is a relationship that is destined for problems— and that includes your relationship with money. So spend (and save) accordingly.

EMOTIONS: WHO'S IN CHARGE OF YOURS?

Knowing God leads to self-control. Self-control leads to patient endurance, and patient endurance leads to godliness.

2 PETER 1:6 NLT

Who is in charge of your emotions? Is it you, or have you formed the unfortunate habit of letting other people—or troubling situations—determine the quality of your thoughts and the direction of your day? If you're wise—and if you'd like to build a better life for yourself and your loved ones—you'll learn to control your emotions before your emotions control you.

Human emotions are highly variable, decidedly unpredictable, and often unreliable. Our emotions are like the weather, only far more fickle. So we must learn to live by faith, not by the ups and downs of our own emotional roller coasters.

Sometime during this day, you will probably be gripped by a strong negative feeling. Distrust it. Reign it in. Test it. And turn it over to God. Your emotions will inevitably change; God will not. So trust Him completely as you watch those negative feelings slowly evaporate into thin air—which, of course, they will.

Our feelings do not affect God's facts.

Amy Carmichael

One thing that is important for stable emotional health is honesty—with self and with others.

Joyce Meyer

Don't bother much about your feelings. When they are humble, loving, brave, give thanks for them; when they are conceited, selfish, cowardly, ask to have them altered. In neither case are they you, but only a thing that happens to you. What matters is your intentions and your behavior.

C. S. Lewis

The spiritual life is a life beyond moods. It is a life in which we choose joy and do not allow ourselves to become victims of passing feelings of happiness or depression.

Henri Nouwen

Character Builder

Remember: Your life shouldn't be ruled by your emotions—your life should be ruled by God. So if you think you've lost control over your emotions, don't make big decisions, don't strike out against anybody, and don't speak out in anger. Count to ten (or more) and take a "time out" from your situation until you calm down.

DAY 60

THE CHARACTER-BUILDING PATH: FOLLOWING HIS FOOTSTEPS

Follow Me, Jesus told them, "and I will make you into fishers of men!"
Immediately they left their nets and followed Him.

MARK 1:17-18 HCSB

Jesus walks with you. Are you walking with Him? Hopefully, you will choose to walk with Him today and every day of your life.

Jesus loved you so much that He endured unspeakable humiliation and suffering for you. How will you respond to Christ's sacrifice? Will you take up His cross and follow Him (Luke 9:23), or will you choose another path? When you place your hopes squarely at the foot of the cross, when you place Jesus squarely at the center of your life, you will be blessed.

The old familiar hymn begins, "What a friend we have in Jesus...." No truer words were ever penned. Jesus is the sovereign Friend and ultimate Savior of mankind. Christ showed enduring love for His believers by willingly sacrificing His own life so that we might have eternal life. Now, it is our turn to become His friend.

Let us love our Savior, let us praise Him, and let us share His message of salvation with the world. When we do, we demonstrate that our acquaintance with the Master is not a passing fancy, but is, instead, the cornerstone and the touchstone of our lives.

Imagine the spiritual strength the disciples drew from walking hundreds of miles with Jesus . . . 3 John 4.

JOHN MAXWELL

Our responsibility is to feed from Him, to stay close to Him, to follow Him—because sheep easily go astray—so that we eternally experience the protection and companionship of our Great Shepherd the Lord Jesus Christ.

FRANKLIN GRAHAM

It's your heart that Jesus longs for: your will to be made His own with self on the cross forever, and Jesus alone on the throne.

RUTH BELL GRAHAM

The Christian faith is meant to be lived moment by moment. It isn't some broad, general outline—it's a long walk with a real Person. Details count: passing thoughts, small sacrifices, a few encouraging words, little acts of kindness, brief victories over nagging sins.

JONI EARECKSON TADA

CHARACTER BUILDER

Following Christ is a matter of obedience. If you want to be a little more like Jesus . . . learn about His teachings, follow in His footsteps, and obey His commandments.

TOO FRIENDLY WITH THE WORLD?

Let no one deceive himself. If anyone among you seems to be wise in this age, let him become a fool that he may become wise. For the wisdom of this world is foolishness with God. For it is written, "He catches the wise in their own craftiness."

1 CORINTHIANS 3:18–19 NKJV

We live in the world, but we should not worship it—yet at every turn, or so it seems, we are tempted to do otherwise. As Warren Wiersbe correctly observed, "Because the world is deceptive, it is dangerous."

The 21st-century world in which we live is a noisy, distracting place, a place that offers countless temptations and dangers. The world seems to cry, "Worship me with your time, your money, your energy, your thoughts, and your life!" But if we are wise, we won't fall prey to that temptation.

If you wish to build your character day-by-day, you must distance yourself, at least in part, from the temptations and distractions of modern-day society. But distancing yourself isn't easy, especially when so many societal forces are struggling to capture your attention, your participation, and your money.

C. S. Lewis said, "Aim at heaven and you will get earth thrown in; aim at earth and you will get neither." That's good advice. You're likely to hit what you aim at, so aim high . . . aim at heaven. When you do, you'll be strengthening your character as you improve every aspect of your life. And God will demonstrate His approval as He showers you with more spiritual blessings than you can count.

Every day, I find countless opportunities to decide whether I will obey God and demonstrate my love for Him or try to please myself or the world system. God is waiting for my choices.

BILL BRIGHT

Christians don't fail to live as they should because they are in the world; they fail because the world has gotten into them.

BILLY GRAHAM

Our fight is not against any physical enemy; it is against organizations and powers that are spiritual. We must struggle against sin all our lives, but we are assured we will win.

CORRIE TEN BOOM

CHARACTER BUILDER

The world makes plenty of promises that it can't keep.
God, on the other hand, keeps every single one of His promises.
If you dwell on the world's messages, you're setting yourself up
for disaster. If you dwell on God's message,
you're setting yourself up for victory.

DAY 62

REBELLION INVITES DISASTER

So roll up your sleeves, put your mind in gear, be totally ready to receive the gift that's coming when Jesus arrives. Don't lazily slip back into those old grooves of evil, doing just what you feel like doing. You didn't know any better then; you do now. As obedient children, let yourselves be pulled into a way of life shaped by God's life, a life energetic and blazing with holiness.

1 PETER 1:13-15 MSG

The Bible means precisely what it says. God's commandments are not offered as helpful hints or timely tips. God's commandments are not suggestions; they are iron-clad rules for living, rules that we disobey at our own risk.

The English clergyman Thomas Fuller observed, "He does not believe who does not live according to his beliefs." These words are most certainly true. We may proclaim our beliefs to our hearts' content, but our proclamations will mean nothing—to others or to ourselves—unless we accompany our words with deeds that match. The sermons that we live are far more compelling than the ones we preach.

So today, do whatever you can to ensure that your thoughts and your deeds are pleasing to your Creator. Because you will, at some point in the future, be called to account for your actions. And the future may be sooner than you think.

The Fall is simply and solely Disobedience—doing what you have been told not to do: and it results from Pride—from being too big for your boots, forgetting your place, thinking that you are God.

C. S. Lewis

If I were asked to formulate as concisely as possible the main cause of the ruinous revolution that swallowed up some 60 million of our people, I could not put it more accurately than to repeat: "Men had forgotten God; that is why all this has happened."

Alexander Solzhenitsyn

We all make messes in our lives through ignorance of God's way.

Joyce Meyer

Obedience is the outward expression of your love of God.

Henry Blackaby

It is the Lord your God you must follow, and him you must revere. Keep his commands and obey him; serve him and hold fast to him.

Deuteronomy 13:4 NIV

Character Builder

Be honest with yourself as you consider ways that you have,
in the last few days, disobeyed God. Then, think about specific ways
that you can be more obedient today.

HUMILITY STRENGTHENS CHARACTER

God has chosen you and made you his holy people. He loves you. So always do these things: Show mercy to others, be kind, humble, gentle, and patient.

COLOSSIANS 3:12 NCV

We have heard the phrases on countless occasions: "He's a self-made man," or "she's a self-made woman." In truth, none of us are self-made. We all owe countless debts that we can never repay.

Our first debt, of course, is to our Father in heaven—who has given us everything—and to His Son who sacrificed His own life so that we might live eternally. We are also indebted to ancestors, parents, teachers, friends, spouses, family members, coworkers, fellow believers . . . and the list, of course, goes on.

As Christians, we have a profound reason to be humble: We have been refashioned and saved by Jesus Christ, and that salvation came not because of our own good works but because of God's grace. Thus, we are not "self-made," we are "God-made" and "Christ-saved." How, then, can we be boastful? The answer, of course, is that, if we are honest with ourselves and with our God, we simply can't be boastful . . . we must, instead, be eternally grateful and exceedingly humble.

Humility is not, in most cases, a naturally-occurring human trait. Most of us, it seems, are more than willing to stick out our chests and say, "Look at me; I did that!" But in our better moments, in the quiet moments when we search the depths of our own hearts, we know better. Whatever "it" is, God did that, not us.

St. Augustine observed, "If you plan to build a tall house of virtues, you must first lay deep foundations of humility." Are you a believer who genuinely seeks to build your house of virtues on a strong foundation of humility? If so, you are wise and you are blessed. But if you've been laboring under the misconception that you're a "self-made" man or woman, it's time to strengthen your character by facing this simple fact: your blessings come from God. And He deserves the credit.

Jesus had a humble heart. If He abides in us, pride will never dominate our lives.

BILLY GRAHAM

It was pride that changed angels into devils; it is humility that makes men as angels.

ST. AUGUSTINE

CHARACTER BUILDER

Remember that humility leads to happiness, and pride doesn't. Max Lucado writes, "God exalts humility. When God works in our lives, helping us to become humble, he gives us a permanent joy. Humility gives us a joy that cannot be taken away." Enough said.

EMBRACING GOD'S LOVE

Unfailing love surrounds those who trust the LORD.

PSALM 32:10 NLT

Have you formed the character-building habit of accepting and sharing God's love? Hopefully so. After all, God's love for you is bigger and better than you can imagine. In fact, God's love is far too big to comprehend (in this lifetime). But this much we do know: God loves you so much that He sent His Son Jesus to come to this earth and to die for you. And, when you accepted Jesus into your heart, God gave you a gift that is more precious than gold: the gift of eternal life. Now, precisely because you are a wondrous creation treasured by God, a question presents itself: What will you do in response to God's love? Will you ignore it or embrace it? Will you return it or neglect it? Will you receive it and share it . . . or not? The answer to these simple questions will determine the level of your faith and the quality of your life.

When you form the habit of embracing God's love day in and day out, you feel differently about yourself, your neighbors, and your world. When you embrace God's love, you share His message and you obey His commandments.

When you accept the Father's gift of grace, you are blessed here on earth and throughout all eternity. So do yourself a favor right now: accept God's love with open arms and welcome His Son Jesus into your heart.

Corrie ten Boom observed, "We must mirror God's love in the midst of a world full of hatred. We are the mirrors of God's love, so we may show Jesus by our lives." And her words most certainly apply to the Christian family, including yours.

God's heart is overflowing with love for you and yours. Accept that love. Return that love. Respect that love. And share that love. Today.

If you have an obedience problem, you have a love problem. Focus your attention on God's love.

HENRY BLACKABY

Even when we cannot see the why and wherefore of God's dealings, we know that there is love in and behind them, so we can rejoice always.

J. I. PACKER

CHARACTER BUILDER

God's love is our greatest security blanket. Kay Arthur advises, "Snuggle in God's arms. When you are hurting, when you feel lonely or left out, let Him cradle you, comfort you, reassure you of His all-sufficient power and love." Enough said.

WITH WISDOM COMES CHARACTER

Do you want to be counted wise, to build a reputation for wisdom? Here's what you do: Live well, live wisely, live humbly. It's the way you live, not the way you talk, that counts.

JAMES 3:13 MSG

D o you place a high value on the acquisition of wisdom? If so, you are not alone; most people would like to be wise, but not everyone is willing to do the work that is required to become wise. Wisdom is not like a mushroom; it does not spring up overnight. It is, instead, like an oak tree that starts as a tiny acorn, grows into a sapling, and eventually reaches up to the sky, tall and strong.

To become wise, you must seek God's guidance and live according to His Word. To become wise, you must seek instruction with consistency and purpose. To become wise, you must not only learn the lessons of the Christian life, but you must also live by them. But oftentimes, that's easier said than done.

Sometimes, amid the demands of daily life, you will lose perspective. Life may seem out of balance, and the pressures of everyday living may seem overwhelming. What's needed is a fresh perspective, a restored sense of balance . . . and God's wisdom. If you call upon the Lord and seek to see the world through His eyes, He will give you guidance, wisdom and perspective. When you make God's priorities your priorities, He will lead you according to His plan and according to His commandments. When you study God's teachings, you are reminded that God's reality is the ultimate reality.

Do you seek to live a life of righteousness and wisdom? If so, you must study the ultimate source of wisdom: the Word of God. You must seek out worthy mentors and listen carefully to their advice. You must associate, day in and day out, with godly men and women. Then, as you accumulate wisdom, you must not keep it for yourself; you must, instead, share it with your friends and family members.

But be forewarned: if you sincerely seek to share your hard-earned wisdom with others, your actions must reflect the values that you hold dear. The best way to share your wisdom—perhaps the only way—is not by your words, but by your example.

When you and I are related to Jesus Christ, our strength and wisdom and peace and joy and love and hope may run out, but His life rushes in to keep us filled to the brim. We are showered with blessings, not because of anything we have or have not done, but simply because of Him.

ANNE GRAHAM LOTZ

CHARACTER BUILDER

Need wisdom? God's got it. If you want it, then study God's Word and associate with godly people.

ASSERTING YOURSELF, PROTECTING YOUR CHARACTER

God doesn't want us to be shy with his gifts, but bold and loving and sensible.

2 TIMOTHY 1:7 MSG

When Paul wrote Timothy, he reminded his young protégé that the God he served was a bold God and that God's spirit empowered His children with boldness also. Like Timothy, we, too, face times of uncertainty and fear in the ever-changing world in which we live. God's message is the same to us today as it was to Timothy: We can live boldly because the spirit of God resides in us.

When your peers encourage you to do things that you know are wrong, are you bold enough to say no? Hopefully so. But if you haven't quite learned the fine art of assertiveness, don't feel like the Lone Ranger—plenty of people, even people who are old enough to know better, still have trouble standing up for themselves.

If you really want to strengthen your character, you have no alternative—you must acquire assertiveness skills. Simply put, assertiveness is an essential component of a strong character. With assertiveness, you can stand on your own two feet; without it, you are doomed to follow the crowd wherever they may choose to go (and oftentimes, they choose to go in the wrong direction).

You're almost never too old to learn how to become more assertive. So do yourself this major-league favor: learn to say no politely, firmly, and often. When you do, you'll be protecting yourself and your character.

Believe in yourself. Have faith in your abilities. Without a humble but reasonable confidence in your own powers, you can't be successful or happy.

NORMAN VINCENT PEALE

Yes, we need to acknowledge our weaknesses, to confess our sins. But if we want to be active, productive participants in the realm of God, we also need to recognize our gifts, to appreciate our strengths, to build on the abilities God has given us. We need to balance humility with confidence.

PENELOPE STOKES

CHARACTER BUILDER

Today, ask yourself if you're being assertive enough at work, at home, or in between. If the answer is no, decide on at least three specific steps you can take to stand up for yourself appropriately, fairly, and often.

CHRIST-CENTERED LEADERSHIP

Those who are wise will shine like the brightness of the heavens, and those who lead many to righteousness, like the stars for ever and ever.

DANIEL 12:3 NIV

The old saying is familiar and true: imitation is the sincerest form of flattery. As believers, we are called to imitate, as best we can, the carpenter from Galilee. The task of imitating Christ is often difficult and sometimes impossible, but as Christians, we must continue to try.

Our world needs leaders who willingly honor Christ with their words and their deeds, but not necessarily in that order. If you seek to be such a leader, then you must begin by making yourself a worthy example to your family, to your friends, to your church, and to your community. After all, your words of instruction will never ring true unless you yourself are willing to follow them.

Christ-centered leadership is an exercise in service: service to God in heaven and service to His children here on earth. Christ willingly became a servant to His followers, and you must seek to do the same for yours.

Are you the kind of servant-leader whom you would want to follow? If so, congratulations: you are honoring your Savior by imitating Him. And that, of course, is the sincerest form of flattery.

True leaders are not afraid to surround themselves with people of ability—and not afraid to give those people opportunities for greatness.

WARREN WIERSBE

The goal of leadership is to empower the whole people of God to discern and to discharge the Lord's will.

STANLEY GRENZ

Leadership is found in becoming the servant of all.

RICHARD FOSTER

The great illusion of leadership is to think that others can be led out of the desert by someone who has never been there.

HENRI NOUWEN

Shepherd God's flock, for whom you are responsible. Watch over them because you want to, not because you are forced. That is how God wants it. Do it because you are happy to serve.

1 PETER 5:2 NCV

CHARACTER BUILDER

In thinking about your leadership style, ask yourself this:
who's your model?
If you're wise, you'll try, as best you can, to emulate Jesus.

KEEPING A PROPER PERSPECTIVE

All I'm doing right now, friends, is showing how these things pertain to Apollos and me so that you will learn restraint and not rush into making judgments without knowing all the facts. It is important to look at things from God's point of view. I would rather not see you inflating or deflating reputations based on mere hearsay.

1 CORINTHIANS 4:6 MSG

For most of us, life is busy and complicated. Amid the rush and crush of the daily grind, it is easy to lose perspective . . . easy, but wrong. When the world seems to be spinning out of control, we can regain perspective by slowing ourselves down and then turning our thoughts and prayers toward God.

The familiar words of Psalm 46:10 remind us to "Be still, and know that I am God" (NKJV). When we do so, we are reminded of God's love (not to mention God's priorities), and we can then refocus our thoughts on the things that matter most. But, when we ignore the presence of our Creator—if we rush from place to place with scarcely a spare minute for God—we rob ourselves of His perspective, His peace, and His joy.

Do you carve out quiet moments each day to offer thanksgiving and praise to your Creator? You should. During these moments of stillness, you will often sense the love and wisdom of our Lord.

Today and every day, make time to be still before God. When you do, you can face the day's complications with the wisdom, the perspective, and the power that only He can provide.

Instead of being frustrated and overwhelmed by all that is going on in our world, go to the Lord and ask Him to give you His eternal perspective.

KAY ARTHUR

Joy is the direct result of having God's perspective on our daily lives and the effect of loving our Lord enough to obey His commands and trust His promises.

BILL BRIGHT

The Bible is a remarkable commentary on perspective. Through its divine message, we are brought face to face with issues and tests in daily living and how, by the power of the Holy Spirit, we are enabled to respond positively to them.

LUCI SWINDOLL

Attitude is the mind's paintbrush; it can color any situation.

BARBARA JOHNSON

CHARACTER BUILDER

Keep life in perspective. Remember that your life is an integral part of God's grand plan. So don't become unduly upset over the minor inconveniences of life, and don't worry too much about today's setbacks—they're temporary.

GETTING TO KNOW GOD BUILDS CHARACTER

Knowing God leads to self-control. Self-control leads to patient endurance, and patient endurance leads to godliness.

2 PETER 1:6 NLT

I f you'd like to strengthen your character, try spending more time really getting to know God. How can you do it? Through worship, praise, Bible study, prayer, and silent meditation.

Do you ever wonder if God is really "right here, right now"? Do you wonder if God hears your prayers, if He understands your feelings, or if He really knows your heart? When you have doubts about your Father in heaven, remember this: God isn't on a coffee break, and He hasn't moved out of town. He's right here, right now, listening to your thoughts and prayers, watching over your every move.

The Bible teaches that a wonderful way to get to know God is simply to be still and listen to Him. But sometimes, you may find it hard to slow yourself down long enough to quiet your mind and tune up your heart. And as the demands of everyday life weigh down upon you, you may be tempted to ignore God's presence or—worse yet—to rebel against His commandments. But, when you quiet yourself and acknowledge His presence, God touches your heart and restores your spirits. So why not let Him do it right now? If you really want to know Him better, silence is a wonderful place to start.

You cannot grow spiritually until you have the assurance that Christ is in your life.

Vonette Bright

Knowing God involves an intimate, personal relationship that is developed over time through prayer and getting answers to prayer, through Bible study and applying its teaching to our lives, through obedience and experiencing the power of God, through moment-by-moment submission to Him that results in a moment-by-moment filling of the Holy Spirit.

Anne Graham Lotz

God wants to be in an intimate relationship with you. He's the God who has orchestrated every event of your life to give you the best chance to get to know Him, so that you can experience the full measure of His love.

Bill Hybels

Character Builder

If you'd like to get to know God a little better,
talk to Him more often. The more often you speak to Him,
the more often He'll speak to you.

THE RIGHT PLACES, THE RIGHT FRIENDS

He who walks with wise men will be wise, but the companion of fools will be destroyed.

PROVERBS 13:20 NKJV

Peer pressure can be a good thing or a bad thing, depending upon your peers. If your peers encourage you to make integrity a habit—and if they encourage you to follow God's will and to obey His commandments—then you'll experience positive peer pressure, and that's good. But, if you are involved with people who encourage you to do foolish things, you're facing a different kind of peer pressure . . . and you'd better beware. When you feel pressured to do things, or to say things, that lead you away from God, you're aiming straight for trouble.

Are you satisfied to follow that crowd? If so, you may pay a heavy price unless you've picked the right crowd. And while you're deciding whom to follow, be sure you're determined to follow the One from Galilee, too. Jesus will guide your steps and bless your undertakings if you let Him. Your challenge, of course, is to let Him.

To sum it up, here's your choice: you can choose to please God first (and by doing so, strengthen your character), or you can fall prey to peer pressure. The choice is yours—and so are the consequences.

You will get untold flak for prioritizing God's revealed and present will for your life over man's . . . but, boy, is it worth it.

BETH MOORE

Do you want to be wise? Choose wise friends.

CHARLES SWINDOLL

There is nothing that makes more cowards and feeble men than public opinion.

HENRY WARD BEECHER

Tell me what company you keep, and I'll tell you what you are.

MIGUEL DE CERVANTES

Those who follow the crowd usually get lost in it.

RICK WARREN

Do not be misled: "Bad company corrupts good character."

1 CORINTHIANS 15:33 NIV

CHARACTER BUILDER

When you're torn between trusting your peers or trusting your conscience, trust your conscience.

MATCHING YOUR ACTIONS TO YOUR BELIEFS

Do what God's teaching says; when you only listen and do nothing, you are fooling yourselves.

JAMES 1:22 NCV

It takes courage to stand up for our beliefs, and it takes character to live by them. Yet far too many of us spend more energy verbalizing our beliefs than living by them—with predictable consequences.

Is your life a picture book of your creed? Are your actions congruent with your personal code? And are you willing to practice the philosophy that you preach? If so, your character will take care of itself.

But if you're doing things that don't meet with approval of the person you see in the mirror, it's time to slow down, step back, and think about how your conduct is shaping your character. If you profess to be a Christian but behave yourself as if you were not, you're living in denial. And denial, in large doses, corrodes character.

So today, make certain that your actions are guided by God's Word and by the conscience that He has placed in your heart. Don't treat your faith as if it were separate from everyday life—instead, weave your beliefs into the very fabric of your day. When you do, God will honor your good works, and your good works will honor God.

Once you have thoroughly examined your values and articulated them, you will be able to steer your life by them.

JOHN MAXWELL

Believe and do what God says. The life-changing consequences will be limitless, and the results will be confidence and peace of mind.

FRANKLIN GRAHAM

God calls us to be committed to Him, to be committed to making a difference, and to be committed to reconciliation.

BILL HYBELS

God delights to meet the faith of one who looks up to Him and says, "Lord, You know that I cannot do this—but I believe that You can!"

AMY CARMICHAEL

Then Jesus told the centurion, "Go. As you have believed, let it be done for you." And his servant was cured that very moment.

MATTHEW 8:13 HCSB

CHARACTER BUILDER

Think about the importance of making your actions conform to your beliefs. Then, ask yourself if your behavior matches your rhetoric. If the answer is yes, congratulations. If not, think of a single step you can take today to stand up for the things you believe in.

WALK IN HIS TRUTH

Jesus answered and said unto him, If a man love me, he will keep my words: and my Father will love him, and we will come unto him, and make our abode with him.

JOHN 14:23 KJV

Elisabeth Elliot advised, "Obedience to God is our job. The results of that obedience are God's." These words serve to remind us that obedience is imperative, but we live in a society that surrounds us with temptations to disobey God's laws. So if we are to win the battle against temptation and sin, we must never drop our guard.

A righteous life has many components: faith, honesty, generosity, love, kindness, humility, gratitude, and worship, to name but a few. If we seek to follow the steps of our Savior, Jesus Christ, we must seek to live according to His commandments.

When we seek righteousness in our own lives—and when we seek the companionship of likeminded friends—we not only build our characters, but we also reap the spiritual rewards that God offers to those who obey Him. When we live in accordance with God's commandments, He blesses us in ways that we cannot fully understand.

Are you ready, willing, able, and anxious to receive God's blessings? Then obey Him. And rest assured that when you do your part, He'll do His part.

The Ten Commandments were given to evoke fear and reverence for the Holy One so that obedience and blessing might result.

Beth Moore

Don't worry about what you do not understand. Worry about what you do understand in the Bible but do not live by.

Corrie ten Boom

Let us remember therefore this lesson: That to worship our God sincerely we must evermore begin by hearkening to His voice, and by giving ear to what He commands us. For if every man goes after his own way, we shall wander. We may well run, but we shall never be a whit nearer to the right way, but rather farther away from it.

John Calvin

God wants man to fulfill His commands as a human being and with the quality peculiar to human beings.

Martin Buber

Teach me Your way, O Lord; I will walk in Your truth.

Psalm 86:11 NASB

Character Builder

Remember this: God has given us His commandments for a reason: to obey them. These commandments are not suggestions, helpful hints, or friendly reminders—they are rules we must live by . . . or else!

CRITICS BEWARE

Don't criticize one another, brothers. He who criticizes a brother or judges his brother criticizes the law and judges the law. But if you judge the law, you are not a doer of the law but a judge.

JAMES 4:11 HCSB

From experience, we know that it is easier to criticize than to correct; we understand that it is easier to find faults than solutions; and we realize that excessive criticism is usually destructive, not productive. Yet the urge to criticize others remains a powerful temptation for most of us. Our task, as obedient believers, is to break the twin habits of negative thinking and critical speech.

In the book of James, we are issued a clear warning: "Don't criticize one another, brothers" (4:11 HCSB). Undoubtedly, James understood the paralyzing power of chronic negativity, and so must we. Negativity is highly contagious: we give it to others who, in turn, give it back to us. Thankfully, this cycle can be broken by positive thoughts, heartfelt prayers, and encouraging words.

As you examine the quality of your own communications, can you honestly say that you're a booster not a critic? If so, keep up the good words. But if you're occasionally overwhelmed by negativity, and if you pass that negativity along to your neighbors, it's time for a mental housecleaning.

We shall never come to the perfect man til we come to the perfect world.

MATTHEW HENRY

Being critical of others, including God, is one way we try to avoid facing and judging our own sins.

WARREN WIERSBE

It was my mother's belief—and mine—to resist any negative thinking.

AUDREY MEADOWS

Positive anything is better than negative nothing.

ELBERT HUBBARD

I have no patience with people who are always raising difficulties.

WINSTON CHURCHILL

If you have a negative thought, don't waste hours thinking about it. Simply direct yourself to something positive and keep repeating the positive until you eliminate the negative.

TINA LOUISE

CHARACTER BUILDER

Negative thinking breeds more negative thinking, so nip negativity in the bud, starting today and continuing every day of your life.

THE SPIRITUAL JOURNEY

Grow in grace and understanding of our Master and Savior, Jesus Christ. Glory to the Master, now and forever! Yes!

2 PETER 3:18 MSG

When it comes to your faith, God doesn't intend for you to stand still. He wants you to keep moving and growing. In fact, God's plan for you includes a lifetime of prayer, praise, and spiritual growth.

When we cease to grow, either emotionally or spiritually, we do ourselves and our loved ones a profound disservice. But, if we study God's Word, if we obey His commandments, and if we live in the center of His will, we will not be "stagnant" believers; we will, instead, be growing Christians . . . and that's exactly what God wants for our lives.

Many of life's most important lessons are painful to learn. During times of heartbreak and hardship, we must be courageous and we must be patient, knowing that in His own time, God will heal us if we invite Him into our hearts.

Spiritual growth need not take place only in times of adversity. We must seek to grow in our knowledge and love of the Lord every day that we live. In those quiet moments when we open our hearts to God, the One who made us keeps remaking us. He gives us direction, perspective, wisdom, and courage. The appropriate moment to accept those spiritual gifts is the present one.

Are you as mature as you're ever going to be? Hopefully not! When it comes to your faith, God doesn't intend for you to become "fully grown," at least not in this lifetime. In fact, God still has important lessons that He intends to teach you. So ask yourself this: what lesson is God trying to teach me today? And then go about the business of learning it.

There is wonderful freedom and joy in coming to recognize that the fun is in the becoming.

GLORIA GAITHER

The whole idea of belonging to Christ is to look less and less like we used to and more and more like Him.

ANGELA THOMAS

God wants to revolutionize our lives—by showing us how knowing Him can be the most powerful force to help us become all we want to be.

BILL HYBELS

CHARACTER BUILDER

Times of change can be times of growth. Elisabeth Elliot reminds us that tough times can lead to a renewal of spirit: "If the leaves had not been let go to fall and wither, if the tree had not consented to be a skeleton for many months, there would be no new life rising, no bud, no flower, no fruit, no seed, no new generation." So remember: Spiritual maturity is always a journey, never a destination.

BEYOND FAILURE

Success, success to you, and success to those who help you, for your God will help you . . . .

1 CHRONICLES 12:18 NIV

Mary Pickford was "America's sweetheart" in the early days of motion pictures. And along with Charlie Chaplin, Douglas Fairbanks, and D.W. Griffith, she formed United Artists Corporation, a Hollywood powerhouse.

Miss Pickford had a simple yet powerful formula for success: She said, "This thing we call 'failure' is not falling down, but staying down." Miss Pickford might have added that every time we get back up, we build character.

Life's occasional setbacks are simply the price that we must pay for our willingness to take risks as we follow our dreams. But even when we encounter bitter disappointments, we must never lose faith.

Hebrews 10:36 advises, "Patient endurance is what you need now, so you will continue to do God's will. Then you will receive all that he has promised" (NLT). These words remind us that when we persevere, we will eventually receive the rewards which God has promised us. What's required is perseverance, not perfection.

When we face hardships, God stands ready to protect us. Our responsibility, of course, is to ask Him for protection. When we call upon Him in heartfelt prayer, He will answer—in His own time and according to His own plan—and He will do His part to heal us. We, of course, must do our part, too.

And, while we are waiting for God's plans to unfold and for His healing touch to restore us, we can be comforted in the knowledge that our Creator can overcome any obstacle, even if we cannot.

Do not be one of those who, rather than risk failure, never attempt anything.

THOMAS MERTON

To have failed is to own more wisdom, understanding, and experience than do those who sit on life's sidelines playing it safe.

SUSAN LENZKES

The difference between winning and losing is how we choose to react to disappointment.

BARBARA JOHNSON

Success or failure can be pretty well predicted by the degree to which the heart is fully in it.

JOHN ELDREDGE

CHARACTER BUILDER

Remember that failure isn't permanent . . . unless you fail to get up.
So pick yourself up, dust yourself off, and trust God.
He will make it right. Warren Wiersbe had this advice:
"No matter how badly we have failed, we can always get up and
begin again. Our God is the God of new beginnings."
And don't forget: the best time to begin again is now.

153

SUBTLE IMMORALITY

For everyone who practices wicked things hates the light and avoids it, so that his deeds may not be exposed. But anyone who lives by the truth comes to the light, so that his works may be shown to be accomplished by God.

JOHN 3:20–21 HCSB

Sometimes sin has a way of sneaking up on us. In the beginning, we don't intend to rebel against God—in fact, we don't think much about God at all. We think, instead, about the allure of sin, and we think (quite incorrectly) that sin is "harmless."

If we deny our sins, we allow those sins to flourish. And if we allow sinful behaviors to become habits, we invite certain hardships into our own lives and into the lives of our loved ones.

Sin tears down character. When we yield to the distractions and temptations of this troubled world, we suffer. But God has other intentions, and His plans for our lives do not include sin or denial.

As creatures of free will, we may disobey God whenever we choose, but when we do so, we put ourselves and our loved ones in peril. Why? Because disobedience invites disaster. We cannot sin against God without consequence. We cannot live outside His will without injury. We cannot distance ourselves from God without hardening our hearts. We cannot yield to the ever-tempting distractions of our world and, at the same time, enjoy God's peace.

Sometimes, in a futile attempt to justify our behaviors, we make a distinction between "big" sins and "little" ones. To do so is a mistake of "big" proportions. Sins of all shapes and sizes have the power to do us great harm. And in a world where sin is big business, that's certainly a sobering thought.

Man prefers to believe what he prefers to be true.

Francis Bacon

What I like about experience is that it is such an honest thing. You may take any number of wrong turnings; but keep your eyes open and you will not be allowed to go very far before the warning signs appear. You may have deceived yourself, but experience is not trying to deceive you. The universe rings true wherever you fairly test it.

C. S. Lewis

There's none so blind as those who will not see.

Matthew Henry

Character Builder

Sometimes immorality is obvious and sometimes it's not.
So beware: the most subtle forms of sin are the most dangerous.

HE IS SUFFICIENT

And He said to me, "My grace is sufficient for you, for My strength is made perfect in weakness."

2 CORINTHIANS 12:9 NKJV

Learning to depend upon God will help you build character. And of this you can be certain: God is sufficient to meet your needs. Period.

Do the demands of life seem overwhelming at times? If so, you must learn to rely not only upon your own resources, but also upon the promises of your Father in heaven. God will hold your hand and walk with you and your family if you let Him. So even if your circumstances are difficult, trust the Father.

The Psalmist writes, "Weeping may endure for a night, but joy comes in the morning" (Psalm 30:5 NKJV). But when we are suffering, the morning may seem very far away. It is not. God promises that He is "near to those who have a broken heart" (Psalm 34:18 NKJV). When we are troubled, we must turn to Him, and we must encourage our friends and family members to do likewise.

If you are discouraged by the inevitable demands of life here on earth, be mindful of this fact: the loving heart of God is sufficient to meet any challenge . . . including yours.

Yes, God's grace is always sufficient, and His arms are always open to give it. But, will our arms be open to receive it?

BETH MOORE

I grew up learning to be self-reliant, but now, to grow up in Christ, I must unlearn self-reliance and learn self-distrust in light of his all-sufficiency.

MARY MORRISON SUGGS

God's saints in all ages have realized that God was enough for them. God is enough for time; God is enough for eternity. God is enough!

HANNAH WHITALL SMITH

God uses our most stumbling, faltering faith-steps as the open door to His doing for us "more than we ask or think."

CATHERINE MARSHALL

CHARACTER BUILDER

If you'd like infinite protection, there's only one place
you can receive it: from an infinite God. So remember:
when you live in the center of God's will, you will also be living
in the center of God's protection.

CONTROLLING YOUR TEMPER

My dear brothers and sisters, be quick to listen, slow to speak, and slow to get angry. Your anger can never make things right in God's sight.

JAMES 1:19-20 NLT

The frustrations of everyday living can sometimes get the better of us, and we allow minor disappointments to cause us major problems. When we allow ourselves to become overly irritated by the inevitable ups and downs of life, we may become overstressed, overheated, overanxious, and just plain angry.

Anger often leads to impulsivity; impulsivity often leads to poor decision-making; and poor decision-making tends to tear down character. So, if you'd like to increase your storehouse of wisdom while, at the same time, strengthening your character, you should learn to control your temper before it controls you.

When you allow yourself to become angry, you are certain to defeat at least one person: yourself. When you allow the minor frustrations of everyday life to hijack your emotions, you do harm to yourself and to your loved ones. So today and every day, guard yourself against the kind of angry thinking that inevitably takes a toll on your emotions and your relationships.

As the old saying goes, "Anger usually improves nothing but the arch of a cat's back." So don't allow feelings of anger or frustration to rule your life, or, for that matter, your day—your life is simply too short for that, and you deserve much better treatment than that . . . from yourself.

Anger is the noise of the soul; the unseen irritant of the heart; the relentless invader of silence.

Max Lucado

Anger unresolved will only bring you woe.

Kay Arthur

Bitterness and anger, usually over trivial things, make havoc of homes, churches, and friendships.

Warren Wiersbe

A man in a passion rides a horse that runs away with him.

Thomas Fuller

Character Builder

If you think you're about to explode in anger, don't!
Instead of striking back at someone, it's usually better to slow down, catch your breath, consider your options, and walk away if you must.
Striking out in anger can lead to big problems.
So it's better to walk away—and keep walking—than to blurt out angry words that can't be un-blurted.

MAKING PEACE WITH THE PAST

Do not remember the past events, pay no attention to things of old. Look, I am about to do something new; even now it is coming. Do you not see it? Indeed, I will make a way in the wilderness, rivers in the desert.

ISAIAH 43:18-19 HCSB

The American theologian Reinhold Niebuhr composed a profoundly simple verse that came to be known as the Serenity Prayer: "God, grant me the serenity to accept the things I cannot change, the courage to change the things I can, and the wisdom to know the difference." Niebuhr's words are far easier to recite than they are to live by. Why? Because most of us want life to unfold in accordance with our own wishes and timetables. But sometimes God has other plans.

One of the things that fits nicely into the category of "things we cannot change" is the past. Yet even though we know that the past is unchangeable, many of us continue to invest energy worrying about the unfairness of yesterday (when we should, instead, be focusing on the opportunities of today and the promises of tomorrow). Author Hannah Whitall Smith observed, "How changed our lives would be if we could only fly through the days on wings of surrender and trust!" These words remind us that even when we cannot understand the past, we must trust God and accept His will.

So, if you've endured a difficult past, accept it and learn from it, but don't spend too much time here in the precious present fretting over memories of the unchangeable past. Instead, trust God's plan and look to the future. After all, the future is where everything that's going to happen to you from this moment on is going to take place.

Shake the dust from your past, and move forward in His promises.

KAY ARTHUR

Whoever you are, whatever your condition or circumstance, whatever your past or problem, Jesus can restore you to wholeness.

ANNE GRAHAM LOTZ

We can't just put our pasts behind us. We've got to put our pasts in front of God.

BETH MOORE

CHARACTER BUILDER

The past is past, so don't live there. If you're focused on the past,
change your focus. If you're living in the past,
it's time to stop living there, starting now.

PROBLEM-SOLVING BUILDS CHARACTER

People who do what is right may have many problems, but the Lord will solve them all.

PSALM 34:19 NCV

Life is an adventure in problem-solving. The question is not whether we will encounter problems; the real question is how we will choose to address them. When it comes to solving the problems of everyday living, we often know precisely what needs to be done, but we may be slow in doing it—especially if what needs to be done is difficult. So we put off till tomorrow what should be done today.

As a person living here in the 21st-century, you have your own set of challenges. As you face those challenges, you may be comforted by this fact: Trouble, of every kind, is temporary. Yet God's grace is eternal. And worries, of every kind, are temporary. But God's love is everlasting. The troubles that concern you will pass. God remains. And for every problem, God has a solution.

The words of Psalm 34 remind us that the Lord solves problems for "people who do what is right." And usually, doing "what is right" means doing the character-building work of confronting our problems sooner rather than later. So with no further ado, let the problem-solving begin . . . right now.

We are all faced with a series of great opportunities, brilliantly disguised as unsolvable problems. Unsolvable without God's wisdom, that is.

Charles Swindoll

Life will be made or broken at the place where we meet and deal with obstacles.

E. Stanley Jones

Each problem is a God-appointed instructor.

Charles Swindoll

Always remember that problems contain values that have improvement potential.

Norman Vincent Peale

Character Builder

Today, think about the wisdom of tackling your problems sooner rather than later. Remember that "this, too, will pass," but whatever "it" is will pass more quickly if you spend more time solving your problems and less time fretting about them.

DISCIPLESHIP BUILDS
CHARACTER

He has showed you, O man, what is good. And what does the LORD require of you? To act justly and to love mercy and to walk humbly with your God.

MICAH 6:8 NIV

When Jesus addressed His disciples, He warned that each one must "take up his cross and follow me." The disciples must have known exactly what the Master meant. In Jesus' day, prisoners were forced to carry their own crosses to the location where they would be put to death. Thus, Christ's message was clear: in order to follow Him, Christ's disciples must deny themselves and, instead, trust Him completely. Nothing has changed since then.

If we are to be disciples of Christ, we must trust Him and place Him at the very center of our beings. Jesus never comes "next." He is always first. The paradox, of course, is that only by sacrificing ourselves to Him do we gain salvation for ourselves.

The 19th-century writer Hannah Whitall Smith observed, "The crucial question for each of us is this: What do you think of Jesus, and do you yet have a personal acquaintance with Him?" Indeed, the answer to that question will determine the quality, the course, and the direction of your life today and for all eternity.

Jesus has called upon believers of every generation (and that includes you) to walk with Him. Jesus promises that when you follow in His footsteps, He will teach you how to live freely and lightly (Matthew 11:28-30). And when Jesus makes a promise, you can depend upon it.

As we seek to become disciples of Jesus Christ, we should never forget that the word *disciple* is directly related to the word *discipline*. To be a disciple of the Lord Jesus Christ is to know his discipline.

DENNIS SWANBERG

There is not Christianity without a cross, for you cannot be a disciple of Jesus without taking up your cross.

HENRY BLACKABY

A life lived in God is not lived on the plane of feelings, but of the will.

ELISABETH ELLIOT

Be imitators of God, therefore, as dearly loved children.

EPHESIANS 5:1 NIV

CHARACTER BUILDER

Today, think of at least one single step that you can take to become a better disciple for Christ. Then, take that step.

BUILDING CHARACTER IN SILENCE

Be silent before the Lord and wait expectantly for Him.

PSALM 37:7 HCSB

Here's a simple little prescription for character-building: carve out a little time for silence every day.

Here in our noisy, 21st-century world, silence is highly underrated. Many of us can't even seem to walk from the front door to the street without a cell phone or an iPOD in our ear. The world seems to grow louder day by day, and our senses seem to be invaded at every turn. But, if we allow the distractions of a clamorous society to separate us from God's peace, we do ourselves a profound disservice. So if we're wise, we make time each day for quiet reflection. And when we do, we are rewarded.

Do you take time each day for an extended period of silence? And during those precious moments, do you sincerely open your heart to your Creator? If so, you will be blessed. If not, then the struggles and stresses of everyday living may rob you of the peace that should rightfully be yours because of your personal relationship with Christ. So take time each day to quietly commune with your Creator. When you do, those moments of silence will enable you to participate more fully in the only source of peace that endures: God's peace.

If the pace and the push, the noise and the crowds are getting to you, it's time to stop the nonsense and find a place of solace to refresh your spirit.

CHARLES SWINDOLL

Silence is as fit a garment for devotion as any other language.

C. H. SPURGEON

Jesus taught us by example to get out of the rat race and recharge our batteries.

BARBARA JOHNSON

Growth takes place in quietness, in hidden ways, in silence and solitude. The process is not accessible to observation.

EUGENE PETERSON

The Lord Jesus, available to people much of the time, left them, sometimes a great while before day, to go up to the hills where He could commune in solitude with His Father.

ELISABETH ELLIOT

CHARACTER BUILDER

Want to talk to God? Then don't make Him shout.
If you really want to hear from God, go to a quiet place and listen.
If you keep listening long enough and carefully enough,
He'll start talking.

HE WANTS TO TEACH

Every morning he wakes me. He teaches me to listen like a student.
The Lord God helps me learn . . . .

ISAIAH 50:4-5 NCV

The Bible promises that God will guide you if you let Him. Your job, of course, is to let Him. But sometimes, you will be tempted to do otherwise. Sometimes, you'll be tempted to go along with the crowd; other times, you'll be tempted to do things your way, not God's way. When you feel those temptations, you must resist them, or else.

What will you allow to guide you through the coming day: your own desires (or, for that matter, the desires of your peers)? Or will you allow God to lead the way? The answer should be obvious. You should let God be your guide. When you entrust your life to Him completely and without reservation, God will give you the strength to meet any challenge, the courage to face any trial, and the wisdom to live in His righteousness. So trust Him today and seek His guidance. When you do, your character will most certainly take care of itself, and your next step will most assuredly be the right one.

God's plan for our guidance is for us to grow gradually in wisdom before we get to the crossroads.

BILL HYBELS

I believe that the Creator of this universe takes delight in turning the terrors and tragedies that come with living in this old, fallen domain of the devil and transforming them into something that strengthens our hope, tests our faith, and shows forth His glory.

AL GREEN

Are you serious about wanting God's guidance to become a personal reality in your life? The first step is to tell God that you know you can't manage your own life; that you need his help.

CATHERINE MARSHALL

We have ample evidence that the Lord is able to guide. The promises cover every imaginable situation. All we need to do is to take the hand he stretches out.

ELISABETH ELLIOT

CHARACTER BUILDER

Would you like God's guidance? Then ask Him for it.
When you pray for guidance, God will give it (Luke 11:9). So ask.

LOVE IS A CHOICE

This is my command: Love one another the way I loved you. This is the very best way to love. Put your life on the line for your friends.

JOHN 15:12-13 MSG

L ove is a choice. Either you choose to behave lovingly toward others . . . or not; either you behave yourself in ways that enhance your relationships . . . or not. But make no mistake: genuine love requires effort. Simply put, if you wish to build lasting relationships, you must be willing to do your part.

Christ's words are clear: we are to love God first, and secondly, we are to love others as we love ourselves (Matthew 22:37-40). These two commands are seldom easy, and because we are imperfect beings, we often fall short. But God's Word commands us to try.

The Christian path is an exercise in love and forgiveness. If we are to walk in Christ's footsteps, we must forgive those who have done us harm, and we must accept Christ's love by sharing it freely with family, friends, neighbors, and even strangers.

God does not intend for you to experience mediocre relationships; He created you for far greater things. Building lasting relationships requires compassion, wisdom, empathy, kindness, courtesy, and forgiveness. If that sounds a lot like work, it is—which is perfectly fine with God. Why? Because He knows that you are capable of doing that work, and because He knows that the fruits of your labors will enrich the lives of your loved ones and the lives of generations yet unborn.

No man truly has joy unless he lives in love.

Thomas Aquinas

It is when we come to the Lord in our nothingness, our powerlessness and our helplessness that He then enables us to love in a way which, without Him, would be absolutely impossible.

Elisabeth Elliot

Love is extravagant in the price it is willing to pay, the time it is willing to give, the hardships it is willing to endure, and the strength it is willing to spend. Love never thinks in terms of "how little," but always in terms of "how much." Love gives, love knows, and love lasts.

Joni Eareckson Tada

To love another person is to see the face of God.

Victor Hugo

Beloved, if God so loved us, we also ought to love one another.

1 John 4:11 NASB

Character Builder

Do you want love to last? Then you must understand this: Genuine love requires effort. That's why those who are lazy in love are often losers in love, too!

GOT STRENGTH?

Create in me a pure heart, O God, and renew a steadfast spirit within me. Do not cast me from your presence or take your Holy Spirit from me. Restore to me the joy of your salvation and grant me a willing spirit, to sustain me.

Even the most inspired Christians can, from time to time, find themselves running on empty. The demands of daily life can drain us of our strength and rob us of the joy that is rightfully ours in Christ. When we find ourselves tired, discouraged, or worse, there is a source from which we can draw the power needed to recharge our spiritual batteries. That source is God.

God intends that His children lead joyous lives filled with abundance and peace. But sometimes, abundance and peace seem very far away. It is then that we must turn to God for renewal, and when we do, He will restore us if we allow Him to do so.

Today, like every other day, is literally brimming with possibilities. Whether we realize it or not, God is always working in us and through us; our job is to let Him do His work without undue interference. Yet we are imperfect beings who, because of our limited vision, often resist God's will. And oftentimes, because of our stubborn insistence on squeezing too many activities into a 24-hour day, we allow ourselves to become exhausted or frustrated, or both.

Are you tired or troubled? Turn your heart toward God in prayer. And while you're at it, pray for the wisdom to simplify your life. When you do, you'll discover that, with God as your partner, you can accomplish the important tasks He places before you today, tomorrow, and every day of your life.

Walking with God leads to receiving his intimate counsel, and counseling leads to deep restoration.

JOHN ELDREDGE

One reason so much American Christianity is a mile wide and an inch deep is that Christians are simply tired. Sometimes you need to kick back and rest for Jesus' sake.

DENNIS SWANBERG

The resurrection of Jesus Christ is the power of God to change history and to change lives.

BILL BRIGHT

CHARACTER BUILDER

Need strength? Let God's spirit reign over your heart:
Anne Graham Lotz writes, "The amount of power you experience to live a victorious, triumphant Christian life is directly proportional to the freedom you give the Spirit to be Lord of your life!"
And remember that the best time to begin living triumphantly is the present moment.

OBSERVING THE SABBATH

Remember the Sabbath day, to keep it holy.

EXODUS 20:8 NKJV

When God gave Moses the Ten Commandments, it became perfectly clear that our Heavenly Father intends for us to make the Sabbath a holy day, a day for worship, for contemplation, for fellowship, and for rest. Yet we live in a seven-day-a-week world, a world that all too often treats Sunday as a regular workday.

One way to strengthen your character is by giving God at least one day each week. If you carve out the time for a day of worship and praise, you'll be amazed at the impact it will have on the rest of your week. But if you fail to honor God's day, if you treat the Sabbath as a day to work or a day to party, you'll miss out on a harvest of blessings that is only available one day each week.

How does your family observe the Lord's day? When church is over, do you treat Sunday like any other day of the week? If so, it's time to think long and hard about your family's schedule and your family's priorities. And if you've been treating Sunday as just another day, it's time to break that habit. When Sunday rolls around, don't try to fill every spare moment. Take time to rest . . . Father's orders!

Worship is not taught from the pulpit. It must be learned in the heart.

JIM ELLIOT

Worship is a daunting task. Each worships differently. But each should worship.

MAX LUCADO

God asks that we worship Him with our concentrated minds as well as with our wills and emotions. A divided and scattered mind is not effective.

CATHERINE MARSHALL

God has promised to give you all of eternity. The least you can do is give Him one day a week in return.

MARIE T. FREEMAN

There is no division into sacred and secular; it is all one great, glorious life.

OSWALD CHAMBERS

CHARACTER BUILDER

Today, think about new ways that you can honor God
on the Sabbath. The Sabbath is unlike the other six days of the week,
and it's up to you to treat it that way.

DOING THE RIGHT THING

Lead a tranquil and quiet life in all godliness and dignity.

1 TIMOTHY 2:2 HCSB

Oswald Chambers, the author of the Christian classic devotional text *My Utmost For His Highest*, advised, "Never support an experience which does not have God as its source, and faith in God as its result." These words serve as a powerful reminder that, as Christians, we are called to walk with God and obey His commandments. But, we live in a world that presents us with countless temptations to stray far from God's path.

Each new day presents countless opportunities to put God in first place . . . or not. When we honor Him by living according to His commandments, we earn for ourselves the abundance and peace that He promises. But, when we concern ourselves more with pleasing others than with pleasing our Creator, we bring needless suffering upon ourselves and our families. Would you like a time-tested formula for successful living? Here is a formula that is proven and true: Seek God's approval in every aspect of your life. Does this sound too simple? Perhaps it is simple, but it is also the only way to reap the marvelous riches that God has in store for you.

So today, take every step of your journey with God as your traveling companion. Read His Word and follow His commandments. Support only those activities that further God's kingdom and your spiritual growth. Be an example of righteous living to your friends, to your neighbors, and to your children. Then, reap the blessings that God has promised to all those who live according to His will and His Word.

The best evidence of our having the truth is our walking in the truth.

MATTHEW HENRY

If we have the true love of God in our hearts, we will show it in our lives. We will not have to go up and down the earth proclaiming it. We will show it in everything we say or do.

D. L. MOODY

For the eyes of the Lord are over the righteous, and his ears are open unto their prayers: but the face of the Lord is against them that do evil.

1 PETER 3:12 KJV

CHARACTER BUILDER

Today, consider the value of living a life that is pleasing to God. And while you're at it, think about the rewards that are likely to be yours when you do the right thing day in and day out.

HOLDING ON TO HOPE

This hope we have as an anchor of the soul, a hope both sure and steadfast.

HEBREWS 6:19 NASB

There are few sadder sights on earth than the sight of a man or woman who has lost all hope. In difficult times, hope can be elusive, but those who place their faith in God's promises need never lose it. After all, God is good; His love endures; He has promised His children the gift of eternal life. And, God keeps His promises.

Despite God's promises, despite Christ's love, and despite our countless blessings, we frail human beings can still lose hope from time to time. When we do, we need the encouragement of Christian friends, the life-changing power of prayer, and the healing truth of God's Holy Word.

It was Jesus who promised, "These things I have spoken unto you, that in me ye might have peace. In the world ye shall have tribulation: but be of good cheer; I have overcome the world" (John 16:33 KJV). This world can be a place of trials and tribulations, but as believers, we are secure. God has promised us peace, joy, and eternal life. And, of course, God always keeps His promises. Always.

Faith looks back and draws courage; hope looks ahead and keeps desire alive.

JOHN ELDREDGE

The hope we have in Jesus is the anchor for the soul—something sure and steadfast, preventing drifting or giving way, lowered to the depth of God's love.

FRANKLIN GRAHAM

I discovered that sorrow was not to be feared but rather endured with hope and expectancy that God would use it to visit and bless my life.

JILL BRISCOE

The Lord is good to those whose hope is in him, to the one who seeks him; it is good to wait quietly for the salvation of the Lord.

LAMENTATIONS 3:25-26 NIV

CHARACTER BUILDER

If you're experiencing hard times, you'll be wise to start spending more time with God. And if you do your part, God will do His part. So never be afraid to hope—or to ask—for a miracle.

# Day 89

The Right Kind of Fear

A simple life in the Fear-of-God is better than a rich life with a ton of headaches.

Proverbs 15:16 MSG

Do you possess a healthy, fearful respect for God's power? Hopefully so. After all, the lesson from the Book of Proverbs is clear: "The fear of the Lord is the beginning of knowledge, but fools despise wisdom and instruction" (1:7 NKJV). Yet, you live in a world that often ignores the role that God plays in shaping the affairs of mankind. You live in a world where too many people consider it "unfashionable" or "unseemly" to discuss the fear of God. Don't count yourself among their number.

To fear God is to acknowledge His sovereignty over every aspect of His creation (including you). To fear God is to place your relationship with God in its proper perspective (He is your master; you are His servant). To fear God is to dread the very thought of disobeying Him. To fear God is to humble yourself in the presence of His infinite power and His infinite love.

God praises humility and punishes pride. That's why God's greatest servants will always be those humble men and women who care less for their own glory and more for God's glory. In God's kingdom, the only way to achieve greatness is to shun it. And the only way to be wise is to understand these facts: God is great; He

is all-knowing; and He is all-powerful. We must respect Him, and we must humbly obey His commandments, or we must accept the consequences of our misplaced pride.

When we fear the Creator—and when we honor Him by obeying His teachings—we receive God's approval and His blessings. But, when we ignore Him or disobey His commandments, we invite disastrous consequences.

The fear of the Lord is, indeed, the beginning of knowledge. So today, as you face the realities of everyday life, remember this: until you acquire a healthy, respectful fear of God's power, your education is incomplete, and so is your faith.

The remarkable thing about fearing God is that when you fear God, you fear nothing else, whereas if you do not fear God, you fear everything else.

OSWALD CHAMBERS

CHARACTER BUILDER

Ask yourself this question: how fearful are you of disobeying God? If the answer is "a lot," you win the prize. But if the honest answer is "not much," then spend a few moments thinking about the potential consequences—perhaps disastrous consequences— that might result from your disobedience.

LISTEN CAREFULLY TO GOD

Trust God from the bottom of your heart; don't try to figure out everything on your own. Listen for God's voice in everything you do, everywhere you go; he's the one who will keep you on track.

PROVERBS 3:5-6 MSG

Sometimes God speaks loudly and clearly. More often, He speaks in a quiet voice—and if you are wise, you will be listening carefully when He does. To do so, you must carve out quiet moments each day to study His Word and sense His direction. And you can be sure that every time you listen to God, you receive a lesson in character-building.

Can you quiet yourself long enough to listen to your conscience? Are you attuned to the subtle guidance of your intuition? Are you willing to pray sincerely and then to wait quietly for God's response? Hopefully so, because the more carefully you listen to your Creator, the more He will work in you and through you.

Usually God refrains from sending His messages on stone tablets or city billboards. More often, He communicates in subtler ways. If you sincerely desire to hear His voice (and strengthen your character), you must listen carefully, and you must do so in the silent corners of your quiet, willing heart.

In the soul-searching of our lives, we are to stay quiet so we can hear Him say all that He wants to say to us in our hearts.

CHARLES SWINDOLL

We cannot experience the fullness of Christ if we do all the expressing. We must allow God to express His love, will, and truth to us.

GARY SMALLEY

When we come to Jesus stripped of pretensions, with a needy spirit, ready to listen, He meets us at the point of need.

CATHERINE MARSHALL

Half an hour of listening is essential except when one is very busy. Then, a full hour is needed.

ST. FRANCIS OF SALES

The one who is from God listens to God's words. This is why you don't listen, because you are not from God.

JOHN 8:47 HCSB

CHARACTER BUILDER

Today, take a few moments to consider the fact that prayer
is two-way communication with God.
Talking to God isn't enough; you should also listen to Him.

REAL REPENTANCE BUILDS CHARACTER

When you are in distress and all these things have happened to you, you will return to the Lord your God in later days and obey Him. He will not leave you, destroy you, or forget the covenant with your fathers that He swore to them by oath, because the Lord your God is a compassionate God.

DEUTERONOMY 4:30-31 HCSB

Who among us has sinned? All of us. But, God calls upon us to turn away from sin by following His commandments. And the good news is this: When we do ask God's forgiveness and turn our hearts to Him, He forgives us absolutely and completely.

Genuine repentance requires more than simply offering God apologies for our misdeeds. Real repentance may start with feelings of sorrow and remorse, but it ends only when we turn away from the sin that has heretofore distanced us from our Creator. In truth, we offer our most meaningful apologies to God, not with our words, but with our actions. As long as we are still engaged in sin, we may be "repenting," but we have not fully "repented."

Is there an aspect of your life that is distancing you from your God? If so, ask for His forgiveness, and—just as importantly—stop sinning. Then, wrap yourself in the protection of God's Word. When you do, both you and your character will be secure.

But suppose we do sin. Suppose we slip and fall. Suppose we yield to temptation for a moment. What happens? We have to confess that sin.

BILLY GRAHAM

Repentance begins with confession of our guilt and recognition that our sin is against God.

CHARLES STANLEY

When true repentance comes, God will not hesitate for a moment to forgive, cast the sins in the sea of forgetfulness, and put the child on the road to restoration.

BETH MOORE

Four marks of true repentance are: acknowledgement of wrong, willingness to confess it, willingness to abandon it, and willingness to make restitution.

CORRIE TEN BOOM

The one who conceals his sins will not prosper, but whoever confesses and renounces them will find mercy.

PROVERBS 28:13 HCSB

CHARACTER BUILDER

If you're engaged in behavior that is displeasing to God, today is the day to stop. First, confess your sins to God. Then, ask Him what actions you should take in order to make things right again.

ACCEPTING LIFE

The Lord says, "Forget what happened before, and do not think about the past. Look at the new thing I am going to do. It is already happening. Don't you see it? I will make a road in the desert and rivers in the dry land."

ISAIAH 43:18-19 NCV

If you're like most people, you like being in control. Period. You want things to happen according to your wishes and according to your timetable. But sometimes, God has other plans . . . and He always has the final word.

Oswald Chambers correctly observed, "Our Lord never asks us to decide for Him; He asks us to yield to Him—a very different matter." These words remind us that even when we cannot understand the workings of God, we must trust Him and accept His will.

All of us experience adversity and pain. As human beings with limited comprehension, we can never fully understand the will of our Father in heaven. But as believers in a benevolent God, we must always trust His providence.

When Jesus went to the Mount of Olives, as described in Luke 22, He poured out His heart to God. Jesus knew of the agony that He was destined to endure, but He also knew that God's will must be done. We, like our Savior, face trials that bring fear and trembling to the very depths of our souls, but like Christ, we too must ultimately seek God's will, not our own.

Are you embittered by a personal tragedy that you did not deserve and cannot understand? If so, it's time to make peace with life. It's time to forgive others, and, if necessary, to forgive yourself. It's time to accept the unchangeable past, to embrace the priceless present, and to have faith in the promise of tomorrow. It's time to trust God completely. And it's time to reclaim the peace—His peace—that can and should be yours.

Prayer may not get us what we want, but it will teach us to want what we need.

VANCE HAVNER

I am truly grateful that faith enables me to move past the question of "Why?"

ZIG ZIGLAR

The key to contentment is to consider. Consider who you are and be satisfied with that. Consider what you have and be satisfied with that. Consider what God's doing and be satisfied with that.

LUCI SWINDOLL

CHARACTER BUILDER

Acceptance means learning to trust God more.
Today, think of at least one aspect of your life that you've been reluctant to accept, and then prayerfully ask God to help you trust Him more by accepting the past.

ACKNOWLEDGING HIS PRESENCE BUILDS CHARACTER

Draw near to God, and He will draw near to you.

JAMES 4:8 HCSB

In the quiet early morning, as the sun's first rays peak over the horizon, we may sense the presence of God. But as the day wears on and the demands of everyday life bear down upon us, we may become so wrapped up in earthly concerns that we forget to praise the Creator.

God is everywhere we have ever been and everywhere we will ever be. When we turn to Him often, we are blessed by His presence. But, if we ignore God's presence or rebel against it altogether, the world in which we live soon becomes a spiritual wasteland.

Since God is everywhere, we are free to sense His presence whenever we take the time to quiet our souls and turn our prayers to Him. But sometimes, amid the incessant demands of everyday life, we turn our thoughts far from God; when we do, we suffer.

Are you tired, discouraged or fearful? Be comforted because God is with you. Are you confused? Listen to the quiet voice of your Heavenly Father. Are you bitter? Talk with God and seek His guidance. Are you celebrating a great victory? Thank God and praise Him. He is the Giver of all things good. In whatever condition you find yourself—whether you are happy or sad, victorious or vanquished, troubled or triumphant—celebrate

God's presence. And be comforted in the knowledge that God is not just near. He is here.

There is a basic urge: the longing for unity. You desire a reunion with God—with God your Father.

E. Stanley Jones

Shake the dust from your past, and move forward in His promises.

Kay Arthur

Claim all of God's promises in the Bible. Your sins, your worries, your life—you may cast them all on Him.

Corrie ten Boom

The next time you hear a baby laugh or see an ocean wave, take note. Pause and listen as his Majesty whispers ever so gently, "I'm here."

Max Lucado

Character Builder

Having trouble hearing God? If so, slow yourself down, tune out the distractions, and listen carefully. God has important things to say; your task is to be still and listen.

OVERCOMING ADDICTION BUILDS CHARACTER

Be sober! Be on the alert! Your adversary the Devil is prowling around like a roaring lion, looking for anyone he can devour.

1 PETER 5:8 HCSB

If you'd like a perfect formula for character destruction, here it is: Become addicted to something that destroys your health or your sanity. If (God forbid) you allow yourself to become addicted, you're steering straight for a tidal wave of negative consequences, and fast.

Ours is a society that glamorizes the use of drugs, alcohol, cigarettes, pornography, and other addictive substances. Why? The answer can be summed up in one word: money. Simply put, addictive substances are big money makers, so suppliers (of both legal and illegal substances) work overtime to make certain that people like you sample their products. The suppliers need a steady stream of new customers, so they engage in a no-holds-barred struggle to find new users—or more accurately, new abusers.

The dictionary defines *addiction* as "the compulsive need for a habit-forming substance; the condition of being habitually and compulsively occupied with something." That definition is accurate, but incomplete. For Christians, addiction has an additional meaning: it means compulsively worshipping something other than God.

Unless you're living on a deserted island, you know people who are full-blown addicts—probably lots of people. If you, or someone you love, is suffering from the blight of addiction, remember this: Help is available. Plenty of people have experienced addiction and lived to tell about it . . . so don't give up hope.

And if you're one of those fortunate people who hasn't started experimenting with addictive substances, congratulations! You have just spared yourself a lifetime of headaches and heartaches.

We are meant to be addicted to God, but we develop secondary addictions that temporarily appear to fix our problem.

EDWARD M. BERCKMAN

Addiction is the most powerful psychic enemy of humanity's desire for God.

GERALD MAY

CHARACTER BUILDER

Remember that ultimately you and you alone are responsible for controlling your appetites. Others may warn you, help you, or encourage you, but in the end, the habits that rule your life are the very same habits that you yourself have formed. Thankfully, since you formed these habits, you can also break them— if you decide to do so.

HARD WORK BUILDS CHARACTER

In all the work you are doing, work the best you can. Work as if you were doing it for the Lord, not for people.

COLOSSIANS 3:23 NCV

The old adage is both familiar and true: We must pray as if everything depended upon God, but work as if everything depended upon us. Yet sometimes, when we are weary and discouraged, we may allow our worries to sap our energy and our hope. God has other intentions. God intends that we pray for things, and He intends that we be willing to work for the things that we pray for. More importantly, God intends that our work should become His work.

Whether you're in school or in the workplace, your success will depend, in large part, upon the passion that you bring to your work. God has created a world in which diligence is rewarded and sloth is not. So whatever you choose to do, do it with commitment, with excitement, with enthusiasm, and with vigor.

In his second letter to the Thessalonians, Paul warns, "if any would not work, neither should he eat" (3:10 KJV). And the Book of Proverbs proclaims, "One who is slack in his work is brother to one who destroys" (18:9 NIV). Clearly, God's Word commends the value and importance of diligence. Yet we live in a world that, all too often, glorifies leisure while downplaying the importance of shoulder-to-the wheel hard work. Rest assured, however, that

God does not underestimate the value of diligence. And neither should you.

It has been said that there are no shortcuts to anyplace worth going. And for believers, it's important to remember that hard work is not simply a proven way to get ahead, it's also part of God's plan for His children.

God did not create you to be ordinary; He created you for far greater things. Reaching for greater things usually requires work and lots of it, which is perfectly fine with God. After all, He knows that you're up to the task, and He has big plans for you. Very big plans.

Chiefly the mold of a man's fortune is in his own hands.

FRANCIS BACON

Help yourself and God will help you.

ST. JOAN OF ARC

Do not be lazy but work hard, serving the Lord with all your heart.

ROMANS 12:11 NCV

CHARACTER BUILDER

Here's a time-tested formula for success: have faith in God and do the work. Hard work is not only the best way to get ahead, it's also part of God's plan for all His children (including you).

SOCIETY'S TREASURES

If you lived on the world's terms, the world would love you as one of its own. But since I picked you to live on God's terms and no longer on the world's terms, the world is going to hate you.

JOHN 15:19 MSG

I t's difficult to race headlong after material possessions and focus on building character at the same time. But, society encourages us to chase a long string of material possessions while paying precious little attention to the accumulation of spiritual rewards.

All of mankind is engaged in a colossal, worldwide treasure hunt. Some people seek treasure from earthly sources, treasures such as material wealth or public acclaim; others seek God's treasures by making Him the cornerstone of their lives.

What kind of treasure hunter are you? Are you so caught up in the demands of everyday living that you sometimes allow the search for worldly treasures to become your primary focus? If so, it's time to reorganize your daily to-do list by placing God in His rightful place: first place.

The world's treasures are difficult to find and difficult to keep; God's treasures are ever-present and everlasting. Which treasures, then, will you claim as your own?

Because the world is deceptive, it is dangerous. The world can even deceive God's own people and lead them into trouble.

WARREN WIERSBE

Every Christian is a contradiction to this old world. He crosses it at every point. He goes against the grain from beginning to end. From the day that he is born again until the day that he goes on to be with the Lord, he must stand against the current of a world always going the other way.

VANCE HAVNER

Rather than being at home in the world, we are continually on the move to something yet undefined.

STANLEY GRENZ

Give me Your grace, good Lord, to count the world as nothing; to set my mind firmly on You and not to hang on the blasting words of men's mouths.

ST. THOMAS MORE

CHARACTER BUILDER

If you're determined to be a faithful follower of the One from Galilee, you must make certain that you focus on His values, not society's values (and by the way, those two sets of values are almost never the same).

GRATITUDE BUILDS CHARACTER

Give thanks in all circumstances; for this is God's will for you in Christ Jesus.

1 THESSALONIANS 5:18 NIV

Sometimes, in the crush of everyday living, we simply don't stop long enough to pause and thank our Creator for the countless blessings He has bestowed upon us.

When we slow down and express our gratitude to the One who made us, we enrich our own lives and the lives of those around us. Thanksgiving should become a habit, a regular part of our daily routines. God has blessed us beyond measure, and we owe Him everything, including our eternal praise.

Are you a thankful person? Do you appreciate the gifts that God has given you? And, do you demonstrate your gratitude by being a faithful steward of the gifts and talents that you have received from your Creator? You most certainly should be thankful. After all, when you stop to think about it, God has given you more blessings than you can count. So the question of the day is this: will you thank your Heavenly Father . . . or will you spend your time and energy doing other things?

God is always listening—are you willing to say thanks? It's up to you, and the next move is yours.

We ought to give thanks for all fortune: if it is good, because it is good, if bad, because it works in us patience, humility, and the contempt of this world along with the hope of our eternal country.

C. S. Lewis

The words "thank" and "think" come from the same root word. If we would think more, we would thank more.

Warren Wiersbe

A sense of gratitude for God's presence in our lives will help open our eyes to what he has done in the past and what he will do in the future.

Emilie Barnes

It is only with gratitude that life becomes rich.

Dietrich Bonhoeffer

Character Builder

Since you're thankful to God, tell Him so.
And keep telling Him so every day of your life.

DAY 98

THE RIGHT KIND OF ATTITUDE

A miserable heart means a miserable life; a cheerful heart fills the day with a song.

PROVERBS 15:15 MSG

Of course you've heard the saying, "Life is what you make it." And although that statement may seem very trite, it's also very true. You can choose a life filled to the brim with frustration and fear, or you can choose a life of abundance and peace. That choice is up to you—and only you—and it depends, to a surprising extent, upon your attitude.

What's your attitude today? Are you fearful, angry, bored, or worried? Are you pessimistic, perplexed, pained, and perturbed? Are you moping around with a frown on your face that's almost as big as the one in your heart? If so, God wants to have a little talk with you.

God created you in His own image, and He wants you to experience joy, contentment, peace, and abundance. But, God will not force you to experience these things; you must claim them for yourself.

God has given you free will, including the ability to influence the direction and the tone of your thoughts. And, here's how God wants you to direct those thoughts:

Finally brothers, whatever is true, whatever is honorable, whatever is just, whatever is pure, whatever is lovely, whatever is commendable—if there is any moral excellence and if there is any praise—dwell on these things" (Philippians 4:8 HCSB).

The quality of your attitude will help determine the quality of your life. So, the next time you find yourself dwelling upon the negative aspects of your life, refocus your attention on things positive. The next time you find yourself falling prey to the blight of pessimism, stop yourself and turn your thoughts around. The next time you're tempted to waste valuable time gossiping or complaining, resist those temptations with all your might.

And remember this character-building tip: You'll never whine your way to the top . . . so don't waste your breath.

The essence of optimism is that it takes no account of the present, but it is a source of inspiration, of vitality, and of hope. Where others have resigned, it enables a man to hold his head high, to claim the future for himself, and not abandon it to his enemy.

DIETRICH BONHOEFFER

CHARACTER BUILDER

Today, create a positive attitude by focusing on opportunities, not roadblocks. Of course you may have experienced disappointments in the past, and you will undoubtedly experience some setbacks in the future. But don't invest large amounts of energy focusing on past misfortunes. Instead, look to the future with optimism and hope.

A REGULAR DAILY DEVOTIONAL BUILDS CHARACTER

Morning by morning he wakens me and opens my understanding to his will. The Sovereign Lord has spoken to me, and I have listened.

ISAIAH 50:4-5 NLT

Do you have a character-building, life-altering, standing appointment with God every morning? Is God your first priority, or you do talk with Him less frequently than that? If you're wise, you'll talk to God first thing every day, without exception.

Warren Wiersbe writes, "Surrender your mind to the Lord at the beginning of each day." And that's sound advice. When you begin each day with your head bowed and your heart lifted, you are reminded of God's love, His protection, and His commandments. Then, you can align your priorities for the coming day with the teachings and commandments that God has placed upon your heart.

Each day has 1,440 minutes—can you give God a few of them? Of course you can . . . and of course you should. So if you've acquired the unfortunate habit of trying to "squeeze" God into the corners of your life, it's time to reshuffle the items on your to-do list by placing God first. And if you haven't already done so, form the habit of spending quality time each morning with your Creator. He deserves it . . . and so, for that matter, do you.

We must appropriate the tender mercy of God every day after conversion or problems quickly develop. We need his grace daily in order to live a righteous life.

JIM CYMBALA

If you, too, will learn to wait upon God, to get alone with Him, and remain silent so that you can hear His voice when He is ready to speak to you, what a difference it will make in your life!

KAY ARTHUR

The greater part of our happiness or misery depends on our dispositions, and not on our circumstances.

MARTHA WASHINGTON

Make your own attitude that of Christ Jesus.

PHILIPPIANS 2:5 HCSB

CHARACTER BUILDER

Get reacquainted with God every day. Would you like a foolproof formula for a better life? Here it is: stay in close contact with God. Hannah Whitall Smith wrote, "The crucial question for each of us is this: What do you think of Jesus, and do you yet have a personal acquaintance with Him?" Think about your relationship with Jesus: what it is and what it could be.

FOR GOD SO LOVED THE WORLD

This is how much God loved the world: He gave his Son, his one and only Son. And this is why: so that no one need be destroyed; by believing in him anyone can have a whole and lasting life.

JOHN 3:16 MSG

Christ sacrificed His life on the cross so that we might have eternal life. This gift, freely given by God's only begotten Son, is the priceless possession of everyone who accepts Him as Lord and Savior. God is waiting patiently for each of us to accept the gift of eternal life. Let us claim Christ's gift today.

God's grace is not earned . . . thank goodness! To earn God's love and His gift of eternal life would be far beyond the abilities of even the most righteous man or woman. Thankfully, grace is not an earthly reward for righteous behavior; it is a blessed spiritual gift which can be accepted by believers who dedicate themselves to God through Christ. When we accept Christ into our hearts, we are saved by His grace.

God's grace is the ultimate gift, and we owe to Him the ultimate in thanksgiving. Let us praise the Creator for His priceless gift, and let us share the Good News with all who cross our paths. We return our Father's love by accepting His grace and by sharing His message and His love. When we do, we are eternally blessed . . . and the hosts of heaven rejoice!

God did everything necessary to provide for our forgiveness by sacrificing His perfect, holy Son as the atoning substitute for our sins.

FRANKLIN GRAHAM

To lose us was too great a pain for God to bear, and so he took it upon himself to rescue us. The Son of God came "to give his life as a ransom for many" (Matt. 20:28).

JOHN ELDREDGE

The essence of salvation is an about-face from self-centeredness to God-centeredness.

HENRY BLACKABY

There is no detour to holiness. Jesus came to the resurrection through the cross, not around it.

LEIGHTON FORD

CHARACTER BUILDER

The time is now. If you have already welcomed Christ into your heart as your personal Savior, then you are safe.
If you're still sitting on the fence,
the time to accept Him is this very moment.

In all things showing yourself to be
a pattern of good works;
in doctrine showing integrity, reverence,
incorruptibility, sound speech that cannot be
condemned, that one who is an opponent may be
ashamed, having nothing evil to say of you.
—
Titus 2:7, 8 NKJV

New Life Ministries

Building Character
and Transforming Lives
Through God's Truth

New Life Ministries is a non profit organization, founded by author and speaker, Stephen Arterburn. Our mission is to identify and compassionately respond to the needs of those seeking healing and restoration through God's truth.

New Life's ministry of healing and transformation includes:

- *❧ **New Life*** – our daily, call-in counseling radio program hosted by Stephen Arterburn. To find a station near you call 1-800-NEW-LIFE or go to www.newlife.com. You can also listen online.
- *❧ **Counselors*** – our network of over 700 counselors nationwide. Call 1-800-NEW-LIFE to find one near you.
- *❧ **Weekend Intensive Workshops***
  - *Every Man's Battle*
  - *Healing Is a Choice*
  - *Lose It for Life*
- *❧ **Seminars***
  - *Reframing Your Life and Love*
  - *Nights of Healing*
- *❧ **Coaching*** – Our personal coaching program is "Professional Accountability" to come alongside you and give you solution-focused direction.
- *❧ **Website***
  - Podcasts and broadcasts of ***New Life***
  - Blogs, message boards and chats
  - Our online store, featuring products by our radio show hosts
  - Find workshops and counselors in your area
- *❧ **24-Hour Call Center*** – There is someone answering calls in our Call Center, 24 hours a day, 7 days a week, 365 days a year.

1-800-New-Life   www.newlife.com

Here is what people are saying...

"I feel better about myself and my life and am now leading a Healing Is a Choice group at my church and helping a group of women to heal! Praise God for New Life Ministries!!!!" - Elizabeth

"My life is changed because I received new insight here into my problem. I know now I am wounded, and I am starting to locate the wound. My life is changed because I have weapons now to fight the enemy of my soul! My life is changed because I now have hope. I have more than hope. I got a promise from God here. He told me, 'I love you. We are going to make it. Don't worry, I know the way home.'" - Brad

"I hear the same relief and hope in the voice of so many of your callers as you dispense your wisdom with down to earth practicality and humor . . . Gradually through your 'voice' and some caring people God placed in my life, I realized he already loved me and had died for me, I had only to accept his gift . . . God bless you and all the others at New Life as you allow yourselves to be an instrument in his awesome hand!"
- Debrah

"From an Every Man's Battle attendee: In one word . . . Amazing! . . . I especially appreciated the 'no holds barred' approach because nothing short of this would have been effective. I never thought I would be able to tell a soul of my struggles, much less a group of strangers, but you made it very doable. Thank you!" - Greg

For information about these and other programs at New Life, please contact us at

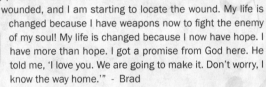

1-800-New-Life   **www.newlife.com**